ADDLESTONE LIBRARY
TEL: 0300 200 1001
WITHDRAWN FROM STOCK
AND OFFERED FOR SALE
WITH ALL FAULTS BY
SURREY COUNTY LIBRARY

WITHDRAWN FROM STOCK
AND OFFERED FOR SALE
WITH ALL FAULTS BY
SURREY COUNTY LIBRARY

Fort Victoria High

1976 to 1983

Barry J Stone

authorHOUSE

AuthorHouse™ UK Ltd.
1663 Liberty Drive
Bloomington, IN 47403 USA
www.authorhouse.co.uk
Phone: 0800.197.4150

© 2014 Barry J Stone. All rights reserved.

No part of this book may be reproduced, stored in a retrieval system, or transmitted by any means without the written permission of the author.

Published by AuthorHouse 06/16/2014

ISBN: 978-1-4969-8316-9 (sc)
ISBN: 978-1-4969-8315-2 (hc)
ISBN: 978-1-4969-8317-6 (e)

Any people depicted in stock imagery provided by Thinkstock are models, and such images are being used for illustrative purposes only. Certain stock imagery © Thinkstock.

This book is printed on acid-free paper.

Because of the dynamic nature of the Internet, any web addresses or links contained in this book may have changed since publication and may no longer be valid. The views expressed in this work are solely those of the author and do not necessarily reflect the views of the publisher, and the publisher hereby disclaims any responsibility for them.

Scripture quotations are taken from the Holy Bible, New Living Translation, copyright © 1996, 2004, 2007. Used by permission of Tyndale House Publishers, Inc. Carol Stream, Illinois 60188. All rights reserved. Website

MEMOIRS OF A TEACHER

The Fort Victoria Years

This is a true account, as true as I remember. The context is a country school in the centre of the country now known as Zimbabwe. About half the pupils were boarders and the rest live in town or close to the town.

Those days were simultaneously fun and sad and often full of the dangers of a bush war against a white minority who had controlled the country since the days of Cecil John Rhodes.

Transition to black majority rule was in the air.

1 Fort Victoria High

"My goodness Norma," I said, "You do look a mess." "So would you, sir, if you had spent the last four hours in a ditch."

It turned out that the bus taking the hockey teams to the Rhodesian Lowveld (lower land countryside in Africa) had been ambushed by terrorists, and all the kids and staff had been pinned down in the ditch by the side of the road for the several hours that it took for help from the military to arrive.

This is the context of some of this book. A country under economic sanctions. A terrorist bush war. Institutions such as schools trying to maintain a normal life. Two sets of so-called independence. Relative peace.

A slow deterioration of a country which had, despite hardships, functioned very well.

Fort Victoria High existed through several Regimes whilst I was there: Rhodesia (under Ian Smith), Zimbabwe-Rhodesia (Under Bishop Abel Muzorewa), back to Rhodesia (with the British flag under Lord Soames), and then Zimbabwe (under Robert Mugabe).

In these accounts I have tended to call the country Rhodesia if it needed mentioning because most of my time was spent in Rhodesia, and because I do not quite remember quite exactly when and in which *'country'* certain events occurred.

The account is not necessarily in historical sequence.

The book is written in sections rather than chapters. This is not a novel, and I deliberately avoided putting 'sections' together. The sections vary in length.

The topics range from harrowing to humorous.

I have had some good editorial assistance from former pupils of the school who have been able to check certain facts. Also old friends who were there.

Any historical or other errors are entirely my responsibility.

Fortunately Norma and the rest of the bus occupants were all safe.

FVH Issues of War

A terrorist war is not a happy thing. It disrupts the lives of many decent people.

Having to take armed convoys at particular times was a nuisance and could be quite frightening. Going without the convoy was worse. I had to do this on one occasion with a colleague and ploughed into a herd of Kudu jumping across the road. This was an unusual event and I assumed the poor animals had been scared out of their habitat and were escaping terrorists. Time to speed up. The car was a wreck, but got repaired. The kudu would have died in pain. The lady passenger had to be taken to the hospital in the next town some miles on. She never travelled with me again. (Why not?)

Hostels had to have high security fences surrounding the property for the protection of the students. The large double gates were locked by sundown. Also a nuisance. There was also training to get under beds at any sign of attack.

The local junior school headmaster was not, apparently, particularly popular. One night we heard a terrific explosion. Under beds!

It emerged that Junior School Headmaster's house had experienced a rocket attack in the night. They missed. All were safe.

I knew his neighbours quite well. Irish extraction. Mrs L's wry dry comment was that it would always take a bomb to get her out of bed.

Fort House backed onto the hospital. From time to time in the early hours of the morning a helicopter would descend upon the hospital with very large webbed sacks slung beneath. It woke the boys who rushed to the windows to see what was happening.

The cold harsh truth was that the sacks contained dead bodies of terrorists. The hospital was the best place to dispense of the bodies. Incineration. We knew there would be smoke from the incinerator smoke stacks that night.

I never revealed this gruesome information to the boys. But some of the older boys knew. And secrets in a small town were difficult to keep.

FVH Ma Scott and Alan

Alan Ferguson was a definitive character. Thin, gangly, full of witty quips. He was much loved by the kids despite his eccentric ways. We became good friends.

Fort Victoria High was a country school far away from other centres. Hence there was a high staff turnover each year. Many first time teachers arrived at the start of the academic year as most were on contract to the government which had supplied them with a generous bursary for four years subject and teacher training. They required three years of service wherever they were posted.

Alan was part of my group of 16 or 18 new teachers. On the first day he settled into an armchair in the staff lounge with a cup of tea and biscuit. And suddenly the imposing, authoritative and intimidating Mrs Scott, who had taught at the school since its opening a couple of decades before, loomed over Alan.

> "I have been sitting in this chair for the last 17 years," she exclaimed.

> "It's about time you had a change then," riposted Alan."

The old staff froze. I don't recall what happened next, but Alan was only one of a few members of staff who was permitted to call 'Ma Scott' by her Christian name, Elise. Even as Superintendent I never ventured that far. It was always Mrs Scott.

Alan used to have competitions among the girls for the most prettiest legs by having them stand on their desks and having the boys judge. In any other circumstances he would not have gotten away with it.

He coached the public speaking teams. On one occasion Alan gave a competent but very nervous contestant a large sherry before she went on. Her opening line was, "Do you have any idea how hard it is to climb three steps when you want to go to the toilet?" She won.

Fort Victoria had no traffic lights, only roundabouts. Alan would frequently go around the roundabouts several times at speed in his white Alpha Romeo before taking the exit to where he was going.

We had a pub at the centre of the school called The Waterhole. Some staff drove there, although the hostels were in easy walking distance. One member of staff who I shall call MG used to get so drunk that we frequently heard him driving around the school grounds trying to find his way to his flat next to the junior hostel.

Alan used to get a little drunk at one of the bars in town, and would arrive back at Fort House, then burst through the front doors singing, "Everybody loves my body sometime . . ." The following morning we would see his car parked in the bushes, not the car park. He was a great source of fun for the boys, and as far as I know they never 'split on him'.

But Alan had arachnophobia. We discovered this when a couple of boys came into the downstairs hostel staff room to show the staff their rather large pet spiders crawling up and down their arms. I was quite glad to see these spiders up close. But we all soon noticed Alan cringing in the corner of the staff room, his escape barred by the spiders and their boys standing near the door. Naturally the boys taunted him by moving closer. Poor Alan.

Poor Alan indeed. Yet I was just as wicked and placed a large rubber spider on the landing of the steps leading down from the first floor to the ground floor where breakfast was being served. Alan started his descent, saw the spider, gave a gasp and froze. I stood with a few of the lads at the bottom of the steps telling him that it was only a rubber spider. It made no difference. Alan stayed put and would have missed his classes had I left it there. So, in compassion and loving kindness I removed it.

We had a couple of slightly bad senior boys in the hostel. Alan's solution was not to give them the cane, but instead to invite and take them for alcoholic drinks at a local hotel. He informed me that he and I would order very low alcohol, large volume Ginger Squares. But the two gentlemen would be encouraged to have much stronger drinks. When they were fairly inebriated we were able to question and counsel them. They realized, 'in their cups', that they had been wrong. That was the end of their nonsense. Kindness and humanness worked better than beatings.

I have since lost touch with Mr Ferguson. I plan to check Facebook. I do know he was an auctioneer with a business in antiques, possibly in Cape Town.

What a character.

FVH Phillip van As

Phillip van As (pronounced ' Fun Us') was a serious minded good decent lad who was also a positive influence in Fort House. He was Afrikaans in background and Afrikaans in nature. I had very little dialogue with him, but always knew he would be kindly there for anyone who needed help. I held him in high esteem.

We never discussed religion, but I think I know that he had been a child of the Most High God for many years. Good upbringing. Obviously much loved by his parents.

And then news arrived that on a weekend stay-over with his grandmother some terrorists had barged into the farm home and shot him and his grandmother dead. There was no apparent reason. He was just a kindly teenager. Why?

Everyone around and about was stunned and shocked. It was very hard for the superintendent to inform the boys in the hostel. It was very hard for me not to weep in public before a hundred kids. And we were seriously angry, wanting to kill. The local farming community was in very murderous mood.

But then there was the reverend Don Enslin. Don married the lovely lady I loved. I went to the wedding. Gillian looked radiantly fabulous. (No regrets. I would have been a perfectly dreadful husband.)

Don was the Methodist minister in town. Phillip van As went to his church, an interesting choice because as an Afrikaner he should have been attending the local Dutch Reformed church.

Don Enslin was a highly perceptive intelligent person. He knew what might happen to local black people in that age and day after the vicious murder and sad funeral of that good boy Phillip. Don was a loving kind nice gentle man and clearly knew right from wrong. He was also tough, bold and strong in mind and speech. No whiff of wimp in him.

Don had been asked to conduct the funeral service in the large Dutch Reform church. It started off routinely with hymns and readings. The boer (farmer) congregation were eager to get the service over with and then get to shooting blacks. They were respectful of protocol, and deeply religious. But bent on vengeance. These were dangerous days.

After the perfunctory pre proceedings Don Enslin started his sermon. He began by starting to read a long Old Testament scripture regarding the fact that only The Lord had the right to vengeance. 'Vengeance is mine, says the Lord.'

Fascinatingly he held up his head and continued, with slow deliberation, quoting from memory the rest of the Divine injunction, looking around and about like the current American president Obama and surveying directly, eye to eye, the congregation. He did not look down at his Bible. He simply dared to challenge the people to accept the Word of God as he quoted that long passage of scripture from memory. I was mesmerised, dumbstruck, and so was everyone else. How could we dare to defy God and take vengeance against innocent people? Large grown men cried in church that day. They knew that the God of Love did not want violence against His children. He alone would deal with the issue of justice.

After that church service nobody was killed. Nobody went out with guns. The healing had begun. One day I will see Phillip again. And so will those Christian farmers.

Don died later in a car crash. A serious loss to the community.

Dear Don, now dead, helped save many people that day, and not just the possible new victims of violence.

I will see him again.

FVH Rat Lab

As the most junior member of staff I was assigned the oldest laboratory. That was where the dissection rats were housed. The place was smelly. Especially in the mornings before the windows were opened to ventilate the place.

Furthermore, the water distiller was in that lab. It supplied distilled water to the other labs, mainly for chemistry classes. The water distiller was noisy.

The cupboards and drawers were labelled with gummed labels. Except they seemed to be disappearing around the edges and had to be replaced regularly.

Then one balmy evening during my first term in Fort House I decided to go to the Rat Lab to mark at the front teacher's bench. It took me away from the noisy hostels, and I was left in peace whilst the duty staff looked after the boys.

After sitting there quietly marking, and as the sounds from the adjacent hostel, Tower House, subsided, I noticed what seemed like rustling from the floor. I stood and peered over the bench. A hundred huge cockroaches on the floor and on the cupboards and drawers chewing around the gummed labels.

Not the squeamish type, I still left by the nearest door. Insects and spiders are the most brilliantly designed animals, and apart from flies, mosquitoes and cockroaches I try to avoid harming them. (Except for button spiders, related to the small Black Widow spider with the red hourglass, and which can be deadly.)

The following evening I returned armed with a can of insecticide spray. As I sprayed these unwelcome invaders instead of running away and dying they began marching towards me. Even the pressure of the spray did not stop them.

I left again hurriedly by the nearest exit.

Between myself and the laboratory technicians we finally got rid of those pesky insects. It meant taking the rat cages out to safety, and using chemical 'bombs'—a common event in Africa.

We could tell they were gone. The labels were no longer disappearing.

FVH The Mayors Car

In the early days roll call in the hostel was only taken once per day. The assumption was that the boys would all be in bed at night. This allowed a 23 and a half hour window for bunking out. Where would the boys bunk to? In town they would soon be noticed since the town had only a junior and a senior school. The town was completely surrounded by bushveld (pronounced *bush felt*). The next nearest centre was 80 miles away by road. There was nothing there anyway.

And then unexpectedly one morning the police arrived to report two boys who had been caught having stolen and driven the mayor's car. The younger boy (about 14) did the driving and his slightly older companion (about 15) was an apparent accessory. One could sit for a driving license at age 16 in those days, so they would not have had theirs. They had driven the car through fields and had damaged the mayor's car. I seem to remember that field was where they were caught.

The hostel superintendent of the day, Roy McCrindle, then instituted two roll calls per day in Fort House, and soon the other hostels followed the practice.

I knew the younger boy's parents from a vegetable shop in Salisbury I helped out friends with on a Saturday mornings, and was therefore a self-appointed advocate for the boy. I was not only naive but rather stupid. Something I regret to this day. That nasty boy was allowed to stay in the hostel at the school after the 'super' had given him six of the best. I shall call the evil boy L.

The older boy was sent to a reform school in Salisbury. I shall call him B. The reform school was run like a prison and no boy was allowed out of the reformatory except under supervision. But he could have scheduled visitors.

B was not well known to me as I only saw him from time to time in hostel, not at school. He appeared to be quiet and gentle and had never caused trouble as far as I understood. I was a little surprised at his behaviour regarding the mayor's car, and somewhat alarmed at his rather harsh sentence. He had no advocate. He would probably have learned his lesson with a whack on his bum and never have repeated such a foolish action. But surely not reformatory.

I should have done more but I was only 24, a Christian with little experience of real life. If it happened today I would fight tough and hard and aggressively and relentlessly for that poor kid. Perhaps he will read this account some day, and perhaps he will contact me, and then I will ask him to forgive me.

In the meantime a profile of L was emerging. He was a small boy but a sinister bully. He was torturing some the younger boys by burning their naked torsos with cigarettes. This was never reported by the victims, and never detected by staff. So called honour among boys never to split on each other, and the younger boys would have been intimidated into silenced.

Eventually that evil lad was discovered and reported by the righteous prefects.

In the meantime I would come out in the morning and find one of the steel hubcaps of my Toyota Crown had been kicked in. It was easy to push out. But this was happening almost irritatingly daily. I wondered who hated me so much as to cowardly attack my car. Furthermore on one occasion I found brown shoe polish on the front left wing of the car. It stained the white paint and that took a little time to get out. Both events turned out to be the evil work of L.

Finally L was expelled, not for the car but for the torture. I should imagine he went on to be a criminal. I now think I know why his parents, who lived in Salisbury, sent him to boarding school in Fort Victoria, 180 miles away.

On a couple of occasions when I had a weekend visit to Salisbury I also visited B at the reformatory. He seemed reasonably fine and bore no malice towards the school. He remained the gentle person I had begun to understand. He was not a criminal, and simply fell under the mesmerizing control of a younger evil lad. B appeared pleased to see me although I sensed some strange unhappiness. I became worried. Something was wrong, but the only reformatory member of staff I managed to engage in conversation revealed nothing.

On the second and last visit I warned B to be careful not to be 'interfered with' by anyone. He knew what I meant. He said he would not engage in homosexual activity, but I saw in his eyes and body language he was. I could not prove it but I knew this gentle soft fifteen year old lad was being sexually abused. It was not possible to pry further. I should have demanded to see the senior supervisor. But I felt so bad and without ability to act. Weak, feeble and useless. All I did was weep. Hence my shame and regrets.

The wrong boy had been sent to the reformatory.

FVH Needing a Wee

Because of our long return trips by bus from rugby matches the lads would need, what was euphemistically known as a 'pit stop'. One aspect of Rhodesia was that all petrol stations had toilets available to clients. So, on one of my early journeys, we stopped at one such station on the way back to the school. It was getting late, and sunset was approaching.

Being naive in the early days to the limitations of one loo per gender we stopped to get relieved at a particular petrol station on the open country road. But two rugby teams were taking a while taking turns to use the facility and we were getting late for supper and parents would be getting anxious. There were no cell phones in those days.

I suggested that the boys also used the ladies room. There would be nobody around. Rural. This speeded things up and the boys did not seem to mind being in the female toilet.

On subsequent trips our pit stops happened along the road. Very little traffic in the country areas, so little chance of being observed, and nobody would have cared anyway. So the guys would all get out of the bus all at one time and wee, backs to the road, against the cattle fence. The only caution was to check that the fence was not electrified (a method of deterring roaming cattle from trying to leave the ranch). Urinating against an electrified fence would not be fatal, but it would be painful.

We made good time after that.

FVH Characters both Teacher and Administration

Most schools are staffed by interesting characters. They are generally teaching because they love the job, love the kids and have a touch of the eccentric—a necessary characteristic for survival.

Unfortunately teachers are underpaid.

We once had to do an audit on our work hours. This included teaching, preparation, marking, clubs, societies, sports, travel and supervision. I worked out that the average good teacher worked a good 25% more than most executives during the year.

And so eccentric characters such as Ian Grant McKenzie came into teaching. He was terribly English gentleman in demeanour and speech. He emanated from a well heeled family and once told me that the only reason he had to work was that his family had lost all their money. It did not stop him driving around in vintage cars, sunglasses and scarf around neck (like Mr Toad in Wind in the Willows) and in a large Mercedes Benz.

And so he opened himself up for ridicule by some staff and much taunting by some pupils. Perhaps they would realize that all the best schools have a variety of different characters, and this is often seen in films.

The kids of Fort Victoria High were generally good, well behaved, kind, loving and obedient. But they were prone to mischief, especially the boys, which I always thought a good thing and which I encouraged as long as no evil was done.

Ian took it upon himself to assist with coordinating morning assembly from time to time. I think he wanted to be perceived at the senior level of the deputy headmistress, Mrs Scott, who when not detained, would usually supervise the assembling of the kids by standing on stage with a stern and frightening visage, saying very little. The idea was to arrange (viewed from the stage) that all boys sat on the left, and girls on the right. The classes sat by class starting with the juniors at the front and ascending to the seniors at the back.

But when Ian was on duty the boys would purposely sit in the wrong row. Ian tried to get them into the correct position by asking whole rows to move into other rows. And so the boys especially deliberately misinterpreted the row and sat in the one either in front of or behind the row they had been told to sit.

As the assembly chaos progressed Ian began to lose his temper and eventually left them to it as Ma Scott entered the back of the hall. Silence fell upon the hall and the boys sheepishly moved into their correct rows.

But they had succeeded in their mission to annoy poor Ian. By the time Mrs Scott had reached the front of the hall the kids had got into their correct position before the staff arrived on stage, along with Ma Scott (who had a heart of gold and compassion beneath the tough exterior) and the Headmaster of the day.

The classes also used to wind up Ian almost every lesson until he lost his temper. I do not know how they did this, but somehow they managed.

But he seemed to enjoy the fun, and would proudly announce, "Well, you know what a temper I have."

Other things happened to poor Ian. He and his wife ran the ballroom dancing class in the school hall. On one occasion he loudly issued a command and his false teeth flew out. Up until that point nobody knew he had false teeth. He immediately strode out the hall leaving his wife to pick up the pieces amidst the uncontrollable laughter of the ballroom club.

His affectations were renowned. He would always want Booths Gin, no other. One evening Jimmy Millar, another wag, was serving behind the Waterhole campus bar. Ian ordered a gin and tonic from the floor and, as always, required Booths—none other. But the Booths had run out and only the empty bottles remained. But there was plenty of Gilberts. I watched as Jimmy quickly decanted half a bottle of Gilberts into the Booths bottle, and then held it aloft pointing at it checking with Ian if that was the right one, which Ian confirmed. And he drank it without murmur. He had no idea that it was not Booths, at least he never said so.

Ian used to get to assembly early so he could sit in the front row near the authority figures. He invariably wore his dark glasses, Mr Toad scarf and crossed his right leg over his left. On one assembly Jimmy and a teacher called Nick sat either side of Ian. Guy Cary, (a member of the English department) always sat down in the hall at the piano, back to the pupils.

Come the prayer of the headmaster, every head bowed and every eye closed, and at the amen the pupils looked up only to see three staff members, Jimmy, Ian and Nick, all wearing dark glasses, all wearing a Mr Toad scarf and all sat with right leg over left. The hall erupted in laughter only to have Guy Cary turn to face the audience, also in dark glasses and scarf. Hysteria reigned for a few minutes whilst Ian had no idea what was going on.

But, as said before, all the best schools have eccentric teachers.

Guy was a character in his own right. He often took part in the plays presented on the town stage—a mile or two from the school. On one occasion at a busy time of the year I heard his motorbike arrive at Tower House where he was superintendent. I couldn't believe it. He was supposed to be on stage. It turned out that his next appearance in the play was about 25 minutes away so he drove back from the theatre to do some work for 15 minutes before returning for his cue to go back on stage.

When I took over as superintendent of Tower House, Valentine Mogg had taken over Fort House where I had first started as a staff member. One unfortunate thing about Fort was that in contrast to Tower's wonderful caring cook matron, the Fort cook matron could not care less. It was just a job to her. She appeared to do as little as possible. One of her quick meals which we seemed to have twice a week was curried eggs and rice—basically boiled eggs in a curry sauce and plain white rice. Hungry boys will eat anything, and since there was no choice we had dormitories filled with 'green gas' two nights a week.

One particular lunch time the senior prefect stood and said the routine grace, "For what we are about to receive may The Lord make us truly grateful." "And forgive the cook matron!" added Valentine in a stage voice which the entire dining hall heard very clearly.

Whilst Fort House had sandwiches at break time, Tower house had a variety of cake. Being in charge of the budget I questioned Marie Louw about the cost of cake. She assured me that cake cost a lot less in terms of ingredients than sandwiches made from bought bread filled with expensive ingredients. So we kept the cake.

One year the five hostel superintendents were given notification of our food budget allowance. Val and I both knew it was too little. We also had government dietary regulations per child. So Val and I spent a Saturday costing out the diet for each boy, item by listed item. This was then multiplied by the number of boys in each hostel and the number of days they would spend in the hostel for the year. Naturally the dietary regulation costings were more than the budget allowed. I told Marie to cook exactly what she thought was good for the kids, and Val and I sent separate letters with the costings to the Ministry of Education. Neither of us heard anything more.

The administration staff had a good relationship the teaching staff, and we all had a lot of fun. Jimmy Miller who was a good friend of one of the secretaries started a habit of whenever she handed him a memo or document, he would in a deadpan glower snatch it out of her hand.

This habit spread to a number of staff and eventually to some of the senior pupils, who thought it hilarious.

The sixth formers also developed an affectation wherein they would not talk to one another unless, foot upturned, their toes were touching. Some of the staff picked up on this and, when talking to the sixth form pupils, also required foot contact.

Roy Jennings, an English teacher, had to have one of the most monotonal boring voices one could imagine. He was a very good fellow, but he had the habit of rambling on and on. The kids nicknamed him Wordsworth. He discovered this and naively thought his love of poetry in his English classes was the reason. I doubt whether he suspected that he talked incessantly. Worse still once within his verbal grasp it seemed that only death could give you release.

One day I needed to talk urgently with a colleague who I knew to be in the staff room. Unfortunately he had been ensnared by Roy, and no amount of gesticulating and attempted interruption would break his verbal chains. So I went to one of the offices and asked to borrow the phone. I called the staff room from the end of the corridor and a colleague answered. I said there is an urgent call for my trapped colleague. At last he was able to break free and we could have our discussion.

Barry Maytham became head during the last few years of my time there. He was a tough man and trucked no nonsense from anyone. There were about four boys who were disruptive bullies. Barry, who had just started as headmaster, expelled them all. The ministry of education office summonsed him to tell him what he had done was illegal, without due process, and that he must reinstate them immediately. Barry's response? Either they go or I go. Barry stayed.

Barry's approach to the school was 'We are the best'. He instituted the regular singing of the tongue in cheek song, "Oh Lord, it's hard to be humble, when you are perfect in every way." Ironically the kids began to believe they were the best. So from a rather mediocre midlands country school we began to rise to the top of the sports league in all sports. We started winning competitions such as the public speaking competition. The whole school gained a new found self respect.

Max Wotherspoon was a gentle teddy bear of a man who obviously loved his job and loved the kids. I never heard him raise his voice. He taught me a few things by example. For instance, one day I was standing next to him and shouting across the field to try to get some obstreperous seniors to do something they were resisting. Having watched me ranting in vain Max gently said to me that I was doing it all wrong. So he showed me how to get those young men motivated to do as they were told by feigning a caning. They obeyed instantly.

Max's real name is Michael. He was nicknamed Max because he gained maximum marks in an IQ test.

Finally, the founder headmaster, Les Sharp. He was only at the school for my first year there, but he was great. All the staff and pupils respected him. Les was quite a small man, but he knew how to lead a school. He had a keen wit and a good sense of humour. Yet few dared to cross him.

On one occasion, when the only way to copy things was on an expensive to run Roneo machine, I wanted a number of pages of an up to date modern biology book copied. They would augment the text book the sixth form was using. It would cost a fair amount. Les Sharp asked me into his office and invited me to justify the expense. Which I did. He authorized the copying. But to this day I suspect that he simply wanted to encourage a young first year teacher and not crush an enthusiastic spirit. He always treated the staff (and pupils) with respect, and staff were seriously valued. This does not happen in some organizations and institutions which are in it for their own glory and for the money. The lesson not understood it seems in certain quarters is that people are the organization's most important assets, and in the institutions in which I have worked where the staff were valued, there was more loyalty, more happiness and more willingness to work hard.

But one of the most memorable things about Les Sharp was his ability to motivate staff who hung around the staff room during tea break once the bell had gone and they needed to get to their lessons. A few seconds after the bell he would whisk into the staff room with the announcement, "Right you are, ladies and gentlemen, I'm afraid that's it."

And off we scuttled.

FVH Bedtime Dorm Checks

One of my daily duties as 'super' was to check that the boys, especially the youngsters, were safely in bed. The seniors were left to themselves because they knew how to behave and when they needed bed and sleep. There was never a problem about sleep for the older lads.

There were regulated times for bed for practical and hostel social reasons. Younger boys would tend to want to mess around in the dorm until late, making them tired and not able to concentrate in school the following day. Other boys did not want fuss and bother when they wanted to sleep. They needed their dorm mates to keep quiet.

My routine on the junior dorm side was to very heavily and noisily slowly bang my way up the wooden stairs. This gave the boys a good warning that the 'super' was arriving. I had no intent to punish those kids, but they needed to get settled to sleep. (I never punished any of them.)

On one occasion as a joke I did what my parents did to me and tucked a young lad into bed. I was playing around, mainly to get the rest of the dorm to have a laugh before sleep.

I never cry in public, even at my beloved and wonderful mother's funeral. But I nearly did weep when I realized that my playful joke of tucking in that fourteen year old boy seemed to mean so much to him. He was missing his family I suspect. He was not interpreting my jest as such, but perhaps thought it was an act of affection. To this day I cannot remember who he is. I was very moved that a simple silly act could have meant what it appeared to have meant to a young man.

More amazing was that when I did final dorm inspection the next day almost all the boys asked to be tucked in. It was a time of pathos. I did it of course and then returned to my flat for a sobbing cry.

FVH War Travel

During the bush war it became routine to travel between towns and cities in convoys in order to increase safety.

Armed vehicles would head and tail each convoy which left Fort Victoria at specific times. If you missed the convoy by a few minutes you had to try to catch it up. The convoy vehicles travelled at speed in order to minimize the chance of being hit by ambush bullets. So the task of catching up took an even higher speed, and quite often it took a long time to catch the convoy.

On one occasion I had missed the convoy and was taking myself and a colleague from Fort Victoria to Salisbury—a journey of about 3 hours. Naturally I travelled at speed. There was only one major town between, Enkledoorn. We were a few miles out of the town. Suddenly a herd of Kudu emerged from the trees on the right and began a high speed run to the other side.

Despite my hard braking and one Kudu's attempt to leap across the car, I hit it. The windscreen was smashed, and the roof buckled. I accelerated because the only thing that could spook those beasts would be the presence of humans—and they may have been terrorists.

After a mile or so my passenger asked me if I was going to attend to her. For the first time I saw that she was covered in shattered glass, and had a few cuts.

I returned to Enkledoorn hospital. A very irritated doctor, who was on a very late lunch break eventually attended to us.

And then again the convoy-less gauntlet. We arrived safely, but she never travelled with me again.

FVH Haircuts at Fort House

One ongoing trouble for the hard pressed boys at Fort Victoria High was haircuts. As a total rebel myself, always resisting a long but always having a short neat haircut, I understood that young gentlemen would prefer a slightly longer cut. (It was the girls, you see.) The evening before the morning hair inspection was an occasion prefects and staff had to sort things out.

Prefects did the trimming. I did the sorting, I made sure the boys looked good, and I was over at the school early the following day to keep the school prefects off my lads. Intimidation. My lads had ensured safety. So I intimidated the prefects.

So the boys were free, neatly trimmed, looking good. Protected. The school prefects did not dare.

In fact the regular hair trims became quite a social occasion. There was the comradeship of all the boys being in the same haircut boat. But it also mean that there was a personal interaction with the prefects, something very important for the juniors.

As superintendent and former house master it was rather important that the young men felt sexually safe. It was a superintendent's duty to check the dormitories morning and evening, but not during bath or shower time. The prefects were responsible for those matters. I made that clear. I never viewed a nude boy in seven years except for the accidental or unexpected times.

On one occasion I was compromised. A young lad who shared my birth date ten years junior summonsed me, via a messenger, to the senior dorm bathroom to sort out the mess his peers had made of his hair. For his protection I will call him CS. His friends insisted that I came to sort out the mess they had made. It was shower time and I was reluctant to go into the dormitory. They almost dragged me in.

CS's hair was a bit of a mess. His friends had made a hash of it. The only best thing was to give him a short trim. CS was a good young lad. Probably about 52 by now.

He was standing there in the nude. A completely nude and naked 15 year old boy. I wanted to go away. I tried to get away. His friends would not allow me to leave. I did not want to let him down. He needed my help. He wanted me to make sensible his hair. He was young and decent lad and needed hair assistance. So I found myself as a housemaster trimming the head of this this bare bodied youth against all my better instincts

And that was that. Never spoken of since.

FVH Hephzibah the Snake

My pet snake Hephzibah (nicknamed Heph) was given to me by a friend of my brother in Salisbury, Rhodesia. He or she was small thin non-venomous constrictor Brown House snake. They appeared to like to live in the safety of houses, hence the name. They are not dangerous.

Hephzibah was only a foot and a bit (35 or so cm) long. Snakes are easy to keep because they do not eat much very often. Fortunately I had been assigned to the so-called rat lab at the school and often had small baby rats to feed Heph. I do not think I would do it these days. Snakes are not as affectionate as dogs or some cats.

Two events come to mind.

In my early teaching years I kept my beard long and bushy. Perversely I took Heph to school one day and hid her in my bushy beard. She or he was quite comfortable there, concealed and warm.

During first break I was chatting to two young lady pupils in the courtyard. Suddenly they moved away and stared at my beard. Heph had been disturbed from her beard nest and had stuck her head out, tongue flickering, to taste what was out there. One has to laugh, but there needed to be an explanation!

However, a more amusing thing happened that morning. I had a free period and popped into the staff room for a cup of tea. D M, the Art teacher, was also there with his cup of tea in hand. Whilst my tea was cooling I wrangled Heph out of my beard and had her snaking around my hand. So I said to D, "Don't you think Hephzibah is looking good?" He answered, "Who is Hephzibah?" So I showed him the snake wrapped around my hand.

He jumped up and away with tea cup smashing to the floor and got himself into the furthest corner of the staff room. I thought that having been born in Africa he would have been used to snakes around and about.

It was only a small harmless little snake.

FVH First Evening Cinema

All the new staff were called together in 1976 by the kindly, but firm, headmaster—Les Sharp, for a pep talk. Part our duties was to supervise Saturday evening cinema shows in the school hall. These were on those old fashioned film reels with a projector.

Most films needed at least one change of reels. At that point the students could go out and take a breather in the balmy air. Of course the film Nicholas and Alexandra took three reels and bored the life out of most of the kids. They seemed glad when it all ended.

Les Sharp insisted that all staff, except for the projector manager, would patrol the surroundings to make sure that there was (in his words) " . . . no fornicating in the 'shrebbery'". That was the way he said shrubbery.

The first time I was duty I was astounded to see all these good looking women arrive in nice dresses. I thought they were party crashes from the town. They were not. The girls were allowed to dress up on film nights. So they did. I am not surprise they wanted to wear something nice. When the school was planned the founder head and his advisor or advisors (I am sure Mrs Scott had something to do with it) decided on the school uniform print for the girls. It was basically vertical white and pale purple stripes. It was most unattractive and was part of a cunning plan to make the girls, even the pretty ones, look like absolute frumps. It was a method of keeping the minds of the lads off the women. So being able to dress up was a treat.

The boys had to wear their school uniform. But were still made to sit on their side of the hall, well away from the now suddenly attractive girls.

No wonder Les Sharp warned the staff to patrol during interval.

FVH Boy with Rash and Wade

A Fort House boy reported a skin rash to the Matron. I checked it out and sent him off to Dr Hampton in town. He came back with some cream.

When I saw the Hamptons at Bible Study later that week I asked Wade what the problem was with the young man and his rash.

"I have no idea," says Wade. So I asked him how he knew what to do. Wade's response was classic. "This week it is the anti-fungal cream. Next week is the anti-bacterial cream. The following week it is the anti-allergy cream. Then the cycle begins again".

I wonder how many GPs operate along similar hit and miss methods.

(Wade is father to my favourite Godson, Matthew.)

FVH Coffee Bar and the Zimbabwe Ruins

A few good people ran a Friday evening coffee bar (Maranatha) near the centre of Fort Victoria. The main objective was to talk to visitors about Jesus Christ. The coffee was good and varied. Some with ice cream, some with marshmallows, some with cinnamon. A local place to go in small town on a Friday night. We used to get some regulars who had nothing much to do at home, and who like a bit of company and cheap nice coffees.

Visitors were a little fewer than our ambitions. On one occasion a certain Alan F, whilst cleaning up the place, jested, "Here I am. Two degrees, and on my knees wiping the floor down."

At one time a conscripted soldier visited, told me his name, and I asked if he knew a professor of the same name at the University of Rhodesia. He did. It was his mother. He was uncomfortable about me outing him regarding his highly respected academic mum in the presence of the other soldiers. I said nothing more. She had lectured us as part of our teaching diploma.

On another occasion a group of soldiers came for coffee and conversation. They were camping and stationed at the notorious Zimbabwe Ruins.

One of the soldiers told me how they all felt the presence of absolute evil emanating from the ruins. They could hardly sleep and had to get away from the evil to our little coffee shop. That information has fascinated me for many years for many reasons. Not least of which was the number of Christians on the school staff. Far greater proportion that in many similar schools.

Zimbabwe Ruins is a jumble of stones piled together in circular constructions. (Google it some time.) Fascinating at first inspection, but actually a shambles. It was where the original Zimbabwe bird carved in stone was found. A strange dark brooding place, even in the bright African sunshine. I rarely visited in the end. Apart from anything it was not exactly easy to walk around.

There are rumours that the ruins were a place of human sacrifice. I cannot find a source for those ideas, hence the rumours remain unsubstantiated.

Having lived in Rhodesia under a number of changing flags we were dismayed at the final Zimbabwe flag.

When I first arrived in Rhodesia we were under the Rhodesian flag which incorporated the Union Flag. UDI had been declared, so got a new Rhodesian Front flag, which ironically incorporated the Zimbabwe bird at the top of the coat of arms. Then the Zimbabwe-Rhodesia flag under the best government the country could have wished under the circumstances. Then back to the British Union flag whilst Lord Soames was Governor overseeing the corrupt elections which brought Mugabe into power.

Then the new Zimbabwe flag.

The main emblem of that current flag is the Zimbabwe bird within a triangle next to the flag pole.

No wonder so much evil has befallen those people. They are stuck in a sort of spiritual dichotomy: On the one hand embracing Christianity. On the other, worshipping their ancestors: Conjuring up spirits of the so-called dead. Spirit mediums going into trances. Witchdoctors who would induce people to die merely by planting the idea into the victim's mind.

There is no way in which one can worship God and have other objects of worship. I just does not work.

There has been a satanic influence over Rhodesia and Zimbabwe for decades. There are many who cannot bring themselves to believe that such dark forces exist. They may not even believe in God. A few months in rural Africa would radically change their perspective.

Going back to the proximity of Fort Victoria High to the Zimbabwe ruins, the proportion of committed Christian teachers at Fort Vic High far exceeded the average for Lowveld schools. Perhaps we were needed there as a spiritual vanguard against the evil of the area.

Winston Churchill (I think) once said that the people get the government they deserve. Zimbabwe-Rhodesians are nice people. Kind, soft and easily intimidated.

A rolling mass action, as happens with South African folk, and the ZANU-PF regime would have gone decades ago.

FVH ESN Kids and Jannie's Mamba

Fort Victoria High School was home to a number of intellectually challenged young people. They were part of the school. It was a progressive idea which I suspect the kindly godly founder headmaster Les Sharp instituted. I have no evidence on that, but it would have been something he would have approved. I last met Les Sharp a FVHS reunion in Johannesburg in or around 1997 or 8. He was looking frail but his mind was spot on. As I write in 2014 he must surely have gone to God.

The technical term for such intellectually challenged pupils was ESN (Educationally Sub Normal). They were all in one class group, age range 11 to 18. The shared task of mostly senior teachers was, essentially, to keep them entertained during school hours and to keep them socialized at other times. And to perhaps teach them something valuable. As an HOD I was commissioned classroom time to look after these loveable young people.

There were three such 'ESN' boys in Fort House when I was house master there. They were what we called in the trade 'good kids'. Not a shred of evil. I will only identify them with letters since by now, if they survived the Rhodesian war, they would be close to their fifties.

If they ever read this book they will know who they are by descriptions and events. J O was a fascinating young man. He found reading (a privilege we who are reading this take for granted) a problem. J was unable to read normal text. But he was able to read aloud his Bible to M H. I have never fathomed that phenomenon. M was another really good kid. I still have a wood tea tray he ornamented in burnt iron and then varnished. One of my treasured artefacts. The third boy A B was a good looking lad, kind, sensible, a friend to his compatriots.

It was A and M who I accidentally caught trying to bunk out of Fort House late one evening after lights out. Bunking was a perennial routine event. My function was to keep the boys safe. Their activity was to thwart that function and go into town whenever possible to do what they wanted. I enjoyed their audacity but I had my responsibilities. A hard caning. Or not. I did not like hitting the kids if I could get out of it.

"Oh Sir, I do wish you had not caught us," said M. Such confession. They both knew that the regulations at that time would be a thorough thrashing. In their honesty I had compassion on them.

I decided not to punish them with a beating. I loved those boys because they were good. Young chaps having a bit of fun? What would God think of me for not being merciful? I suggested they went back to bed, and left it at that. Zero punishment.

J was a very nice considerate young man. I was living in a cottage next to the Junior hostel. Sunday (or was it Saturday?) afternoon J O visited holding a Green Mamba snake (*Dendroaspis augusticeps*). Mambas are deadly and quite common in that area. One strike and you are possibly dead. Green Mambas are as venomous as Black Mambas—both common to that region.

I was shrinking back into my settee saying to J that I thought it would be a good idea if he took the snake outside. J told me how he seen the mamba (tree living snake) coming towards him out of the corner of his eye when he was exploring in the bush. As mentioned before J was not a fool, just fractionally reading and writing impaired. (Remember he could read the Bible.) He had snatched by the neck the Mamba he espied by his peripheral vision out of the tree before it had got to him. Surely his Angel was looking after him.

J O took the Mamba away, back to the bushveld, and we both lived. So did the snake.

FVH Max Wotherspoon

Max Wotherspoon was the definitive school master. He was kind, considerate and cared for the kids. I rather hope that he and his wife and children think of me fondly from time to time. I taught his son some science. Such a sensible lad. He must be in his late forties by now.

In my early days at Fort Vic High I was rather overbearing. Pushing my way around. Being harsh on the children. Totally wrong and totally unbecoming. Generally proud, arrogant, conceited—and those were just my good qualities.

Max taught me good things.

One sport afternoon whilst I was ranting at some rambunctious boys Max quietly suggested that I calm down a little. He advised me how to deal with naughty boys. Without any fuss he called to them and simply feigned a caning. The boys understood. They must have loved him for that.

Max apparently got the name 'Max' because he had, in his youth, gained the maximum mark in some sort of test. I never found out about that test. His real name is Michael.

His laugh was very distinctive and always made the kids (and some staff) snigger. He sort of laughed backwards, drawing in air through his larynx instead of pushing it out.

He later became a very good headmaster.

FVH Breakdown in the Lowveld and loss of Convoy

On one occasion I drove the school minibus and team to a rugby match in the Lowveld. We travelled, uneventfully, with the armed convoy.

On the return trip, as we reached the main road north to Fort Victoria I realized that the right front brake was seizing. I stopped the bus on the side of the road. The convoy swept on ignoring the possible plight of 16 schoolboys and their teacher.

At that time we were not being issued automatic guns by the police. But I had borrowed a World War 2 Luger from a colleague. I took it out and wondered if it was operational. So I fired it into the dirt at the side of the road. It was a scary moment for me and the boys, alone and with one gun. Despite being an inter-town road, there were few vehicles at any time, let alone during the war. And the next (and last) convoy was not due for a couple of hours.

Of course, later, I realized that I should never have fired it. It could have alerted the enemy to our presence. And we were one bullet down.

The front right brake was very hot. We had limited water on board, and I wished to conserve that for the radiator. So, one by one, the boys and I urinated over that brake hub. It did the trick.

We were on our way again on a very nerve wracking journey home.

FVH Helping the Choirs

Maisie Wilson was a wonderful Scottish lady. She was always helping the school choirs in their musical productions and was an excellent choir mistress for local adult productions in Fort Victoria.

On one occasion I was passing the main hall where Maisie was struggling with a group of junior girls on a choral item. She had all the girls behind her as she sat at the piano, back to the main entrance.

Because she was frequently stopping playing to give the girls help and instructions I snuck into the hall and crept up behind those girls. They did not notice me. Too focussed on their difficult task of getting both music and words together and in harmony.

In those days I, being a young man, I could sing—within a range—soprano. So I joined in and bolstered that little team of struggling young ladies. Things improved. Their confidence seemed to grow, and before long they were getting the music right. Maisie could play on.

Unfortunately one girl spotted me out of the corner of her eye—perhaps me being tall gave the clue. She saw me singing along with soprano voice and was reduced to a fit of giggles. All the girls turned to the giggler, saw me, and also began to laugh. Maisie turned around in irritation asking what was going on in her shrill Scottish accent. She saw me: I waved 'Hi', and slunk out.

Nothing more was said, even at our own choir practice of Bach's St John's Passion later that week.

The boys also had singing as a 'rounding out' subject, and three male teachers staff trained them. (And, most importantly, kept them in order!)

Ed Smith (a diminutive Canadian) played the music on Guitar, Barry Percival kept discipline, and I conducted with a comb.

We were rehearsing an old American song (name forgotten) with the final line of the verse was,

> "Rolling. Rolling.
> Rolling down the River."

The boys were getting the 'Rolling, Rolling' bit right. But getting the timing on 'Rolling down the River' was a little tricky. Ed played and sang it. "Dun Dun Dun Dun Duuu-Ner". The boys tried it. Wrong again. Ed again, "Dun Dun Dun Dun Duuu-Ner". The boys tried it again, and again were all out of synchronization.

After Ed had run through it a few times without success, I stepped in with my comb.

I sang it with my comb baton attempting to beat out the timing. "Da Da Da Da Daaaaaa Da".

I repeated this a few times, baton comb flying in the air, and then asked the boys to try it.

Once. Didn't get it.

Twice. A bit better.

Thrice. By this time I was gesticulating wildly with my comb, brought too close to my face where it caught in my bushy beard and stayed there.

The boys fell about in hysterics at this spectacle, and all the staff, self included, joined in the laughter.

Having had a good laugh, and now considerably less tense, the choir finally got the timing of, "Rolling down the Riiii-ver" correct.

FVH Lindy Black

Lindy Black was a sweet, kind sophisticated slender young lady who spoke very good English. This came from her parents, who lived in town, and who were amateur thespians.

Lindy was much loved by staff who were very fond of her. She was always polite. She deported herself well. And she worked hard.

Then one day she was missing from my science class. I knew she was in the school, so I asked the class where she was. Apparently with the headmaster. I could not think why, but I never asked.

About ten minutes into the lesson she arrived. As she entered some of the boys did some gentle ragging and mocking.

"Don't **fuss** with **me**," she said. "I am not **in** the mood." The boys instantly fell silent. She glided to her seat and sat down. And that was the end of the matter.

I still laugh out loud to this day 30-something years later when I remember that incident.

FVH Drunk at the piano

Men in Rhodesia in the late nineteen seventies of the last millennium had to do military service. We were trained in the use of guns, the wearing of uniforms, the code of conduct when using the radios, and other crushingly tedious pointless routine drills.

Not exactly my scene. I hated the war. I did not agree with the government. I did not see why we should be in a civil war against mainly good African people. I hated the experience with tear gas. Rather nasty stuff, rather cruel, rather wicked. Possibly necessary at times, but never nice.

I hated being a young man naked in the communal shower with other older naked men looking at me. I hated the crude rude unnecessary language of crude rude useless so-called 'army' men who were no more men than (in Sean Connery's phrase in a film than my bum was a banjo.) What would their wives think? I hated the whole shocking lot. But by law we were compelled to do military service and kill if necessary. I never did. Would not, could not. Except for self defence. It did not happen. So I am innocent of murder.

I was useless at hitting a target with a rifle. I almost managed to give the soldier next to me more hits on his target for which he did not have sufficient ammunition. I was pathetically useless, but I was still very bold and brave. I was rarely afraid. This is not a boast. My care free attitude was not my own doing. The Lord God Most High was looking after me, and if I got killed I would go to Him. I just knew that my family would mourn a great deal so tried to remain circumspect and alive.

For a certain season we teachers had to patrol the neighbouring black 'township'. It is still a mystery why. The patrols took place at night. No sleep, no brain function. The people in control never seemed to think of that. It messed with our lives and messed with our teaching. Little sleep, brain confused, confused pupils. Those kids seemed to understand. They were kind to us. They did not mess with us, even though we could barely function.

A strange phenomenon about duties patrolling the local 'township' was that got to learn where we were by recognizing the lights. And then we were ordered to do a daylight patrol. None of us had a clue where we were.

Then on one occasion I was not sure if my rifle was on safe mode or not. I knew how to put that rather powerful rifle on and off safe, but did not know which way was which. So I pointed up unto the air and pulled the trigger. It was not on safe and made a terrific noise as I let off a round.

The next day I was hauled into the commander's office. He was angry with me, but I could not care at that stage. I did not remember any instruction on that rifle. Besides, what could he do to me, a civilian?

Then there was a holiday call up. As soon as school ended the next day I was due for duty at a place called Devulie bridge to protect it from terrorists getting across the river at that point. So Alan gave me whiskey that afternoon. (I could kill him for that.) He gave me a great deal of whiskey. I don't remember even going to bed. Dead dreadfully dangerously drunk.

The following morning I was due to play the assembly hymn. The usual piano player was already on call up. I was so overhung I hardly saw the piano let alone the music sheet. It was a hash. I made an absolute fool of myself. All the wrong chords and notes. But nobody said a word. Not the kids. Not the staff. Not the headmaster of the day, Roy McCrindle. He must have known. Or perhaps he did not want to believe it.

That was clear love and kindness by kind kids and colleagues. I could have hugged them all.

Next, into the bush to dangerous Devuli with serious threat of death.

FVH Orange Wine

Boys will and should be boys. I think it is important that boys get up to good mischief. It develops their manhood. It develops their masculine leadership. Of course they need to know the difference between right and wrong and certainly not be downright evil. But there is good mischief in the sense that nothing evil is done, just a bending of rules. A sense of good fun.

Having some risky good fun is to be encouraged. The young men will have good memories to share with their grandchildren. Grandchildren enjoy true stories and can learn good things from them. (Sons and daughters are rarely receptive to the rants of their parents. A wanton waste of wisdom.) But never underestimate the good that grandparents bring. Eventually the son, a little older and a little wiser, will take heed of his mum and dad.

An annual event at Fort Victoria High School was the 'Leaver's Ball'. The ladies and gentlemen who had just written their final exams would be treated to food, fun and dancing. They were served by the students one year below them. The servants would be the masters the following year. This was an event attended by most staff.

This excellent occasion left all the other hostel dwellers unsupervised except by a skeleton staff—one per hostel. We were therefore not witness to the fun since we had duties and responsibilities. *In loco parentis.*

In or around the 1980 ball I was supervising both adjacent boy's hostels. It meant a regime of walking through the dormitories of Tower House, then walking through the dormitories of Fort house, then walking through the dormitories of Tower House again, and then walking through the dormitories of Fort House, again. They needed a presence. I was it. It was tiring, but the next day was not a school day and I could rest. Deep and dreamless sleep.

Except that on my rounds I caught a whiff of alcohol. That would be a '*situasie*' (situation) needing resolution. I think that in those days I had a sense of what problems alcohol could cause in the future. That sense of problems of alcohol has been evident all around me in the year of The Lord 2014. Many of my vast family of uncles, aunts, cousins, and second cousins have had struggles with alcohol with relatives and friends for decades.

But I was concerned in 1980 for those kids. I knew and loved most of them from both hostels.

Thus began the inquiry stroke inquisition. Some of the chaps had been brewing a sort of alcoholic wine drink, in secret, using freely available inexpensive oranges. Such imagination and ingenuity. Also chemically suspect. I would have rather bought them a beer or two than let them drink such potentially dangerous undistilled chemical concoctions which could have contained any number of different alcohols, including methanol.

A dozen or so boys were brought before me, confessing their sins. They knew they could not lie to me and in any case most were brought up to tell the truth. I had to appear to be uncompromisingly harsh and used tough words of reprimand. Stone, the ogre.

Inside myself I admired them, and of course loved them. They were, at heart, good kids. Up to good mischief. But needing a little protection. How could one punish them for a prank?

I never reported a single one of them, and none of them received a caning.

FVH Bus Crash

One of the most dreadful things to happen in any school is for pupils to die or be killed.

In or around 1981 the news reached me in Tower House hostel that the big school bus had overturned some miles from Fort Victoria.

I asked a couple of prefects to come with me and we sped to the accident site. The bus was upside down in the ditch on the right hand side of the road—opposite to the side traffic travels in Zimbabwe. There were vehicles around. Almost all of the pupils had been taken back to town by families and friends to be treated at the hospital—mostly for minor things. There was not much else I could do, except there was a rather dazed and shocked-looking Tower House boy called Rogerio who seemed to be aimlessly wandering around. He had not been taken back by the convoy of cars which had come to assist.

I offered to take him back to Tower and he resisted. He was clearly rather scared to travel in any vehicle. It took some persuasion to get him into the Merc and I remember I took it gently on the journey back.

He was rather dirty with dust from the crash so I asked a couple of his friends or prefects—I forget which—to help him take a bath in my superintendent's bathroom. He needed the comfort of the other boys whilst he calmed down a bit.

I went around to the hospital (the school, hospital and police camp were on the same island of land within the roads which went around). Two of my Tower boys were there—one of my best prefects, André, with one ear half torn off. Another, Wayne Barbour, had his leg in plaster—fractured femur. A young chap, John Kennedy, had also died. He was a good lad. Here is an insert from one of his friends, more than 30 years later:

> "I DO remember the bus crash (of '81, I think), where both Wayne Barbour and John Kennedy (amongst others) died. It was particularly difficult for me at the time, since John and I were the 2 'reserves' on the A team, and he was chosen to go instead of me . . . As you can imagine, my young mind and heart had trouble getting around that little piece of "destiny"! But, as I mentioned in a previous email, you were a great help to many of us in that difficult time, and even FORCED (kinda?) us to "deal with it" more fully than we "tough young men" might have wanted to (just avoiding the idea, escapism, etc.) . . . If memory is correct on this one, you actually pulled a bunch of our class (is that right? or was it another group?) out of something we should have been doing (classes temporarily suspended? Homework time? Not sure what it was . . .), brought us into your flat, and played that 2nd movement of Beethoven's 5th Piano Concerto (leaving hardly a dry eye in the room) . . . Few words were spoken, but much grief healing was started right there. That's the kind of guy you were, and only the Lord knows how many lives you touched with that kind of compassion and (on-purpose) interest in the welfare of the kids in your charge . . ."

Upon returning to the hostel I phoned both their parents to reassure them that their son's were fine.

Wayne's dad wanted to immediately drive up from the Lowveld, a couple of hour's journey, in his fast Jaguar. I knew hard working Alan Barbour well enough to know that he would be very tired, would drive too fast, and it being dark would be in serious danger of colliding with a cow (they tended to wander onto the road at night when the barbed wire fences had a gap). I suggested he drove up in the morning in the light of day.

Early the following morning just after 6 am, before the boys were up, I received a call from the hospital. Wayne had died in the night from complications. I was devastated. I phoned Alan to tell him the sad sad news, but had no information as to why or what complications had occurred. I have since regretted discouraging him from driving up, but I had not expected a young lad to die from a broken leg.

Next, in tears, I found myself wandering into the deserted morning foyer of the hostel. Wayne's name was on the signing out board along with the names of all the other boys. I took it down. And then thought better of it. I replaced his name, and awaited roll call to tell the hostel. Many of the boys became visibly upset. His friends could hardly believe it. I was dumb with disbelief.

It was clearly the fault of the relatively incompetent nursing night staff. Zimbabwe had arrived. The beginning of the end of all that was good in Rhodesia, starting with the hospitals. With a fractured bone there is a danger that some bone marrow would enter the bloodstream and end up either clogging a heart artery or a brain artery. Both can be fatal. Standard treatment with such a bone break in those days was to administer a dilute alcohol drip which would effectively dissolve the rogue bone marrow. The doctor may have forgotten to prescribe this, and the nurses clearly had no idea or did not care. Only a white boy. I was angry, and not very polite to the hospital staff.

I spoke with André who was in the same ward and he told me that Wayne began to have breathing difficulties in the night. He raised the alarm, but by the time anyone got there it was too late.

I wept every day for a fortnight or so within my flat. I tried not to show it, but I reckon one or three prefects coming on official hostel business saw that I had been crying, despite my efforts to wipe away my tears and blink away my probably red eyes when I heard the knock at the door. They were polite enough to never mention my grief—at least not to me. What I really needed was a hug from them, but that was not appropriate for a prefect to hug their Superintendent. I know that other boys and lads in the hostel also wept for poor Wayne.

Wayne's funeral was a melancholy affair, attended by many people. His ashes were taken to the peninsular island owned by the former Mayor of Fort Victoria and his wife—mutual friends of Alan and me. I forget which of the other pupils were there. I assume his friends.

Nobody knew why the bus veered across the road only to overturn in the ditch. The driver was killed. He had no alcohol in his bloodstream. He was a religious man. The autopsy revealed no evidence of a seizure or heart attack. He was a loyal, faithful and competent driver. Only in Heaven will we be able to find the answer to that mystery. There was nothing found wrong with the bus. All school vehicles were very well maintained.

Three young girls died in that crash. Their crushed bodies were found under the bus—they had been thrown out just before the bus rolled onto them. Barry Percival, a colleague, was at the scene when the bus was lifted up. He said they looked pathetically like squashed rag dolls.

Our school had messages from other schools who had had similar tragedies. But for many of us the memories of what was one of the worst days of our lives still haunt us.

Barry Maytham

Barry Maytham was a tough new headmaster. I really hope he is alive and well and might read this account.

There were many aspects needing credit to him. He informed the school that they were the best. They believed him, and the staff started to believe him. An excellent leader. A tough kind man with a wonderful sense of humour. He was good to the staff and good to the kids. But very tough. Good job too, as my deceased mother would say.

He ensured that we sang good things to that effect at morning assembly services. I do not know whether he was a Christian, but I hope so.

We are the best, he refrained. We became the best school in the region because of his encouragement. He saw us through some difficult times. Another section.

He had two children at the school. I taught one of them. She was fantastic. A child I would have wanted for myself.

He was a head teacher that was not intimidated by anyone. Not even the lovely frightening Ma Scott. Certainly not the local ministry of Education. Barry feared nobody.

We had some rather rotten teenage boys who were causing heartache and hurt among the good lads of the school. Barry Maytham expelled them. He was summonsed to the Education ministry in Fort Victoria town. Reinstate the bullies was the command. Barry Maytham simply said that if they come back I leave. Bold. Brave. Beautiful. The ministry folded. Barry Maytham stayed on. The bullies never came back. Sometimes we need to be really bold and very tough.

We had a few ex patriot drug running Australian staff who arrived and were pushing marijuana. I discovered this and reported it post haste. I wanted those so-called teachers out of my hostel and out of my boy's lives.

Barry Maytham got rid of them so fast it could have been done with mirrors.

Thus endeth my tribute.

FVH *The Bomb*

The male school staff were called up before so-called Zimbabwe independence by the military to perform certain policing duties. Technically we were police reservists. However our uniform was army camouflage.

News from rural nuns was being reported that whole villages were being wiped out by Mugabe's forces.

They killed men, women and children without mercy. The worst thing about those events was that we were powerless to prevent it. Terrorism is a terrible thing.

R G Mugabe has already gone down in history, and history will judge him. Hence international condemnation, and heavy economics by all but a few countries, and of course travel bans for him and many of his ministers.

He has reportedly enriched himself with funding meant to help the Zimbabwean people. He has overseen and condoned the most terrible torture of Zimbabweans. A sixteen year old schoolboy at a Catholic school close to Mugabe's official residence dared to criticise the government. That boy was taken into custody, stripped naked, and tortured mercilessly with electrodes to his genitals. Cruelty. May God have mercy on their souls.

Although I did not know the rebellious Prime Minister Ian Smith my father did. Ian Smith intended good I suspect. Perhaps a little misguided. But he lived in a modest home close to Salisbury and therefore close to government buildings. He drove himself to work in an old beat up Mercedes Benz (always a good vehicle for the farm). I knew this as a fact because I had passed him on his way to work driving in opposite directions in the city.

When Mugabe came to power road travel became a major event. People nicknamed him as Bob Mugabe and the Wailers. Plenty of police, military, cars, motorbikes screaming into town exceeding the speed limit just to get to his office. Many people died in those parades. We knew of at least one old couple unable to immediately to quickly enough discern that the 'president' was en route. They were shot to death in their small car. Many fast moving motorbike riders died whilst manoeuvring around traffic.

Mugabe manipulates parliament in order that there is little possible opposition. Already he wants to remove the brave MDC (opposition) prime minister. Morgan Tsvangiria's wife was killed in questionable circumstances. The regime reportedly stole food aid from the external donors, who apparently found other way to get assistance to the general poplace.

History could have been changed.

Margaret Thatcher and Ronald Reagan could have avoided the institution of the evil regime by not forcing the Lancaster House talks. It was rumoured that R G M had given up the terrorist fight and so was surprised at the invitation to talks.

The outcome of the talks were and are a national disaster. Another election, barely a year after the good functioning rule of Bishop Abel Muzorewa and his excellent cabinet of ministers. Muzurewa died in exile in 2010.

Our school staff men were called up to supervise local polling stations for a second time. It did not take long to realize that R G M was intimidating the populace. The election which brought R G M into power was declared relatively free and fair, but was an unhappy farce. Living in a small town means that one gets to meet all sorts of people, including the police commissioner. He was not shy in telling us that despite the reports of the election being free and fair it was not. Britain wanted the problem to go away. I wonder whether Margaret Thatcher ever knew the extent of the intimidation and the extent of the killings. Villagers were told that ZANU would know how people voted. The people, unused to sophisticated elections, believed this lie. It was impossible to know and impossible to vote more than once.

Most ironically there was an assassination attempt on Mugabe close to Fort Victoria. He was campaigning (intimidating) in the area. We heard the bomb go off from the airport region at the hostel. I took a wonderful young lad, Glen Stevens, out to the bomb site to see what happened. Glen was around about 16 years of age, but a little small for his age. He had diabetes. He also had a sense of humour, and never complained about his affliction. He was a favourite among the staff. He died young. I will see him in heaven.

I have a photo of him standing in the crater in the road made by a pipe bomb under the road designed to explode as Mugabe's car took him to the local airport.

The bomb was detonated one or two seconds too late. Mugabe survived. Zimbabwe has not.

FVH Walking into Grandma's House

There was one especially naughty boy in Fort House. His grandmother lived in town, an easy walk from the hostel. This chap was constantly bunking out of hostel. The staff, being in *loco parentis*, had the task of recovering him. It was not difficult to work out that he would usually be at grandma's place.

On one occasion when the boy was missing from hostel I drove into town, parked a little up from the house, and let myself into the front door. In those days people did not often lock their doors, and grandma knew me well enough.

I sneaked around the house hoping to catch him in the act of bunking.

I opened one door, a bedroom door, only to encounter a naked couple interrupted in the middle of raunchy sex. I simply apologised and quickly shut the door. I had no idea who they were and never, until now, mentioned it to anyone.

I recovered the boy, drove him back to the hostel and gave him the cane.

FVHS Smoking

Smoking was not allowed at the school. It was illegal anyway, but also a school rule that smoking was not allowed. It seems to be a general international school rule for good reason. I have observed certain 'ladies' walking to Magna Carta school (UK 2011) puffing away whilst walking to first classes. Having 'taught—i.e. supervised there briefly' I remember the twin odours of nicotine and peppermint swirling around the girls. Strangely no such smoke detection among the boys. Although to my astonishment whilst driving to that school I saw a mother (I assume) lighting a fag for her fifteen year old son. She needs to be pilloried, although I doubt she would know the meaning of the word.

Back to Rhodesia. I am very sensitive to cigarette smells. The boys knew that. School staff were on the alert all the time. Most of the pupils at Fort Victoria High School did not smoke. There was, to my knowledge, no drug problem except for a little alcohol. They were good kids. Nice kids.

A small few boys had got into the smoking habit. Also good kids. Ironically they were the younger boys. But I later learned that to avoid detection they sneaked down to the sport field changing room with a bag. They would then strip naked, put their clothes in the bag, and light up. The bag was to avoid cigarette smoke getting into their clothing. Having hurriedly finished their cigarette they would put their clothes on and try to return to the hostel undetected. I wonder why they bothered. It would have been easier to have given up smoking.

The most surprising revelation was that one of the best prefects of Fort House told me just before he left school to go to university that he had been a secret smoker. Had he been found out he would have be fired from his prefect post.

That would have been a real tragedy as he was a really excellent hostel help.

FVH Riding Shotgun

In those days (1978 to around 1980) the teaching bus driving staff were armed with automatic machine guns. These were signed out from the Fort Victoria police station on the day of the sports match.

Many of the kids lived on farms and were boarders at the school and were quite used to guns and the terrorist threat. As a member of staff driving the bus it would have been extraordinarily tricky (what were they thinking?) for the driver to drive and simultaneously handle a machine gun, so I always handed mine to the most competent boy on board (usually Hendrick Spies) the bus who then rode shotgun. Most of these farm lads were well practiced in the use of weapons, and thought nothing of taking responsibility for covering the bus in the event of an ambush.

It was a comfort to us all that I was not responsible for fending off an ambush, and we all trusted lads like Hendrick to be able to shoot straight.

FVH The Van Der Graaff Joke

One of the experiments the kids loved involved the Van de Graaff static electricity generator.

We had just had a fun lesson with the year three science class where one by one each pupil put a hand on the static generator metal sphere to see whether their hair would become charged enough to stick up. And we all held hands to see whether the charge went between us, which it did. It was important to be wearing rubber-soled shoes, which school shoes were. But there was an insulating mat to stand on for individuals.

As the generator was used, the belt became more charged and the static voltage quicker to form, especially in the dry season. And of course there were the usual tricks using another smaller metal sphere to see how large a gap a spark could be made to jump. Plus the soft fibre 'brush' which could be plugged into the top and the fibres made to stick up and apart as they became charged with the same polarity which made them repel each other.

It was this phenomenon which caused a wicked plan to hatch in my mind. I let the year threes into the scheme, and they co-operated.

The Van de Graaff generator was placed alongside me behind the front desk and on the insulating mat. The water still (used to provide contaminant free water for the laboratories)was turned on in order to make some cover noise. The fume cupboard fan was switched on to add to the cover noise so that the noise of the generator was not so easily discerned.

I stood behind the desk, generator running, one hand on the metal dome, and the other on the wood bench top. This allowed charge to leak through my body and away, thus I was not charging up. The year threes left by the doors at the back of the lab and looked suitably miserable whilst a couple of three muttered to the awaiting year twos that Stone was in a dreadful mood and not to mess with him today.

The year twos came in sheepishly and I glowered at them. "Sit!"

Then the act.

"Your homework," I said, without elaborating. (There was nothing wrong with their homework. They were good kids.)

I continued on in a harsh tone, picking fault, and removing my hand from the wood bench. I felt my hair—which was longer and fuller than it is now—start prickling and rising up. I watched those poor kids looking at my hair watching it happening. And when it was as charged as it could be I almost shouted that this was something I would tolerate, and slapped the bench. Instant discharge, and shock on their little faces as my hair fell flat. I did the performance once more, hair charged, then discharged.

I could not let them suffer any more, and laughed and told them that this was a joke and that their work was fine and they were good pupils. Relief.

And then instead of my planned lesson, I brought the Van de Graaff generator and mat out to the front bench and we played until the end of the lesson. They and I had a good laugh and great fun.

31 FVH Scabies

One weekend morning Sick Bay Matron came to me with a concerned expression. One of the boys had a rash on his wrist which she thought might be scabies. Scabies is caused by a mite, is highly contagious, and very uncomfortable in a warm climate.

I had the town doctor have a look at it and he confirmed scabies and told me to send the boy home. By that time several other boys were exhibiting the same symptoms, so I sent them home.

News soon spread that if you had scabies you could go home. Of course, at that time, I was young and naive, and certainly not medically trained. What I had seen on the diagnosed boys was what seemed to be tiny red pinpricks on their wrists.

I have since learned that the scabies mite can infect a number of areas of the body, but in my naivety failed to check these out. I have also learned that this affliction is quite easily treated with certain modern creams and lotions, but the town doctor prescribed nothing.

Initially, about seven boys were sent home. But then there came a 'rash' of other boys displaying similar pinprick symptoms on the insides of their wrists. What could I do but send them home too. I could not take chances with the rest of the hostel.

I began to suspect that the apparent rashes were self inflicted, but had no proof, and the boys were not going to tell.

Eventually about a third of the hostel went home. It became quite a peaceful place.

FVH The Vodka Experiment

The science curriculum we used in the lower high school was designed to maximize useful education. It was also designed to be interesting and fun. And it was designed by the staff of the school. Improvisation often occurred to augment the learning experience.

With the fun and useful factors in mind I decided to demonstrate the effects of alcohol consumption on reaction times with a view to discouraging drink driving in later years. (Most of the boys, and many of the girls were driving cars, tractors and 'bakkies' on the farms since they were 8 or 10 years old. My youngest niece would drive her mother's Mercedes SLC on the road to visit an old family friend. She was only 15 at the time. Thus are some of the freedoms of Africa.)

The reaction time experiment was simple, as was the apparatus. A wood metre rule. A bottle of Vodka. Three children. A teacher. Observers—i.e. the rest of the class.

This was not an experiment where the pupils would be allowed to drink alcohol, so I was the guinea pig. In addition, this experiment had to take place during the latter half of the last period of the day before luncheon. Should I become inebriated it would be wrong for me to try to teach.

Method: Two pupils were to record the experimental results. One child was to hold the end of the metre rule vertically the bottom end just level with the thumb and forefinger of the teacher.

The class had gathered around to watch. The ruler was released without warning at the discretion of the ruler holder. The teacher had to close his digits thereby catching the ruler as it slipped between his thumb and first finger. The reading on the ruler where it was caught was then recorded on the blackboard.

The teacher then drank a double Vodka and the experiment repeated. Unfortunately his reactions appeared to be just as good on the second test as with the complete sobriety test.

Another double. The third test. Similar results. No noticeable change in reaction time.

Last Vodka. Experiment number four. Little reaction change.

And then the final bell went. The kids went to their homes and hostels, and I packed my briefcase, locked the laboratory doors on my way out, and went over the Fort House hostel for lunch, feeling none the worse for wear after three double Vodkas.

It was the superintendent's duty day. His name is Roy McCrindle, a really nice gentle kind man with a tendency to suddenly drop off to sleep in the middle of a conversation. Roy was sitting at the head of table and I was next to him that day. Food was served, and we began to eat.

Suddenly and unexpectedly the room began to swim and I felt quite giddy. The Vodka had finally kicked in. I said nothing after that wave of drunkenness started swirling around me.

To this day I do not recall what happened thereafter, but I know that if I was coaching sport that afternoon I would have made a complete hash of it.

That was the first and last time I tried that experiment.

FVH The Love of Fun

We all loved fun. Boys and men love fun. So it was that Frodo Mogg and I took some boys from Fort House on a Saturday to the wonderful splendid lake Kyle and settled on the mucky muddy side. No crocodiles there. Just dirt. Safe. We would never put our lads in danger.

Val Mogg and I sat on our camping chairs and laughed loudly whilst the boys frolicked in the mud in their underpants. It was a very daft and silly event. Val and I drank tea whilst enjoying the warm African sunshine. Knowing that our staff would be looking after our hostels. The boys were mucking each other around with mud. They had a great deal of frolic and fun. Just as God intended.

By time to return for supper the fun loving boys ran into the lake, washed off all the mud, dried off in the sunshine, got dressed and did not soil our motor cars for the return journey. They were considerate polite lads. Easy to love.

That was a nice fun day for nice kids. And much fun for the superintendents.

FVH Viscount Flights

In the late seventies the standard passenger plane for Air Rhodesia was the now obsolete propeller driven Viscount.

These were slow planes which could not fly very high. By today's standards they would probably not been allowed to start up let alone fly.

Two Viscounts had been shot down by terrorists. A number of passengers survived the second crash. But they were executed in cold blood by the terrorists who had tracked the descent of the crippled plane. Two witnesses survived to tell the tale.

So Air Rhodesia decided planes should fly at very low levels—a few hundred feet about the tree tops. I was on such a plane flight with a rugby team. It was considered safer than going by bus and risking ambush.

The flight was exciting and interesting, but potentially dangerous. One gust of wind could have caused those old unsophisticated machines to plough into the ground.

Air Rhodesia decided to change its flying methods. After take-off, the plane circled their towns and cities with airports until they reached their maximum possible height. The idea was that towns like Fort Victoria were surrounded by farmlands and therefore unlikely to harbour terrorists with round to air rockets. At the end of the journey the planes spiralled down to the airport. That manoeuvre added extra time to the journey. And the planes had to have engines on full power for the whole flight, the cabin very noisy and the nose pointed upwards for the whole journey.

It could have done those engines no good.

FVH The Madness of Dangerous trips

Despite the bush war most schools still engaged in sports and other competitions. Despite the potential danger of being attacked by armed terrorists there was an attitude that the terrorist war was not going to affect the normal routine—especially the routine of playing sports in other towns and cities.

The routine was that the evening before the trip the staff in charge of teams would go to the police station and sign out an automatic weapon. We were expected to drive the bus and be ready to grab the gun and shoot back in the event of an ambush.

I realized that this would be very dangerous, so I routinely handed the gun to Hendrick Spies (pronounced 'Speece and in Fleece) who at the tender age of 15 was very mature and was destined to become of Fort House's best prefects. He rode shotgun whilst I drove the bus as quickly as possible.

The reader needs to know that in Rhodesia the towns are far apart, hundreds of kilometres in most places.

So when we played a school match in the Lowveld south of Fort Victoria we would have several hours to travel. On a particular occasion, before it became routine to sign out a weapon from the cop station, I had to make such a trip down. So I borrowed and old German Luger from Alan Ferguson.

We caught the convey down to the Lowveld (pronounced low-felt). These were scheduled to depart from town at specific times. They comprised an armed vehicle at the front and another at the rear sporting a powerful cannon gun. The cars and minibuses drove between the military vehicles. Travel speed was maximum—no speed limits.

The return journey was not as smooth. About a quarter of the journey home the bus developed a seized front right wheel. For some reason the brake was not released on that wheel, and the vehicle was experiencing speed and driving difficulties. I had to stop the bus on the side of the road. The convoy sailed past and the team and I were left alone. The front right wheel was red hot, and the brake pads stuck. I decided we had to wait until the drum cooled down a little.

I took Alan's gun out. I was not sure which way the safety catch went. Foolishly I failed to warn the boys when I fired a shot into the ground. The safety was off and the gunshot was loud. I still regret the added stress to the already alarmed boys. It was a stupid thing to do as it could have alerted terrorists if they were in the area.

We had to do something about the wheel. There was some water in the bus, but it was not enough to cool the brake drum enough the release the brake. One by one the boys urinated onto the wheel. I was the last to go. I was praying that we could get on the road again soon, and God answered those prayers.

We boarded the bus and drove off at top speed. There was no chance of catching the convoy, and I avoided using the brakes—not difficult on long open empty roads. We arrived some time later at the school, tired, relieved and thankful.

Over 30 years later I still wonder why we took so many risks for the sake of sport. Madness.

FVH Two Brothers and a Father with Brain Cancer

There were two brothers in the new junior hostel Les Sharp House. I had moved to one of the four junior hostel flats as part of now being slightly senior staff before signing up as superintendent of Tower House. I got to know two young brothers in that hostel. They were very disturbed and unhappy boys—family problems. I wondered why they were staying in the hostel in any case since their grandparents owned a spacious house in town—easy walking distance to school.

I learned that these boys had a father in a medical facility in a town 100 miles away. This was a mental hospital dealing with difficult mental patients. He had brain cancer and had been prevented by their misguided (in my opinion) and rather stubborn cantankerous grandparents from having visits by his two sons. This decision was seriously hurting those two boys, who were old enough, being at high school, to understand things. The boys really wanted to see their father, as did he presumably did them. That mental hospital was a couple of hours away by car.

So I hatched a risky plan to sign out the brothers from Les Sharp hostel on a Saturday morning, and drove them to their dad. He was locked up, and getting through the security arrangements meant some smart talking.

When we arrived at the door in the section he was staying, he recognized his boys through the bars in the door window, and in a tone of amazement called their names. "Is that really you?" he said.

It broke my heart to see those two boys and their dad reunited after so long. Dad and sons were all crying. A member of sanatorium staff then supervised the visit in another, more congenial room. I decided to get out of the way and sat in the car. And also wept whilst listening to the Beethoven Violin Concerto.

Quite a while later the brothers emerged and got into the car. The journey home was fairly solemn, and few words were spoken. The boys thanked me several times. I had bought them luncheon before we set out for Fort Victoria.

Dad was dying when he met his sons for the first time in several years. It was the last time they ever saw him. He died soon after our visit. He is now long dead. The brothers are now in their late forties, possibly with wives and children. Their grandparents are probably deceased or very very old.

I do not regret acting illegally regarding these youngster. It was against their grandparents' wishes. Sometimes illegal actions (according to government) is not illegal according to God. Just think how those lads would feel all their lives having not seen their dad before he died.

And I do not even remember their names.

FVH Skiing in Austria

Ma Scott arranged a 10 day holiday taking in some skiing in Austria and a short tour of Italy. Her husband Cecil were to be the main leaders and organizers of the trip, for which they received their own holidays free.

Three other staff went along, self included, and about 20 pupils. The airline was Air Zambia, which was one of the cheapest carriers at the time.

First stop, Lusaka International Airport—an experience not to be missed, or repeated.

Most of us felt the need for the loos. These were in the main foyer, and catered for men and women, and were not separated.

There was a process here. First find a cubicle with a door. If one was fortunate it had a lock, but most did not. Then try to find a loo with a seat. A door and a seat was relatively essential. But then the toilet paper. There were none I found with door and seat and toilet paper. So one had to hunt for toilet paper in one of the doorless or seatless cubicles. They tended to have toilet paper since few people used them. So, toilet roll in hand, back to the cubicle with a seat and a door without a lock. Locking was a foot against the door.

The airport was almost deserted. As we arrived a team of customs officers suddenly appeared. Our stop over was a few hours so we had to enter the country officially in order to climb aboard two rickety old buses and head into Lusaka for brunch. That was another journey not to be missed or repeated.

Lunch over, back to the airport and back on the plane. We had an uneventful flight to Austria. The contrast between Zambia and Austria was striking. Fourth world to First world.

We had five days to learn to ski and then attempt the easy route down Mount Titlis (the boys were amused by the name: the girls were not). The ski instructor was a hunk and had the girls virtually swooning over him; attention he appeared to enjoy.

The main skill was to know how to slow down on the snow and perhaps stop. We were shown the moves. Then onto the cable seats—which were more difficult to negotiate than expected. I fell off at first attempt thereby causing the entire set of seats to be stopped so I could climb aboard.

At the top of the lift we were unceremoniously pitched off onto a down ramp made of ice due to a thousand compactions per day. Now to get down. I noticed that the stop manoeuvre did not seem to work very well so employed the method of falling to the side onto the snow. This basically carried on all down the slope.

At one point on the way down when I was beginning to travel faster than I wanted to a sudden hump appeared in direct line. I could not slow down and ended up doing my first involuntary ski jump.

At the bottom of the slope I was met by M who took one look at me and packed up laughing. I asked her what was so funny. "Look at yourself!" she exclaimed. I was covered in compacted ice and snow. I looked like a Yeti.

The youth hostels we stayed in were Spartan but adequate. We tended to eat out, and merely slept there. However, the place was under-ventilated and over-heated. So we opened the windows a crack at night. The proprietor discovered this and she was furious. She had paid money for the heating and we were letting it seep away. We asked for the heat in our small dormitory to be turned down.

Midnight Christmas Mass at a wonderful old church was inspirational even though it was mostly in German. We knew the music, and were able to sing along in English.

On our last day of skiing training which came as part of the package tour a few of us decided to risk going to the top of Mount Titlis and trying out the easy slope down. I was relieved, initially, when only a few of us were in the cable car. Then the doors to the platform opened and a hundred skiers crammed themselves into the car. We were squeezed together, and I grew anxious about the weight. As we ascended I nervously looked down to the green ice below us. I was glad we were skiing down, and not using the cable car.

At the top we located the easy route. The two other routes were intermediate and advanced. Each route was indicated by coloured poles in the snow, so we knew which way to travel. It was beautiful up there. At one point we seemed to be walking across a flat area which I was told was a frozen lake covered in snow. I wondered how a lake would form so high up.

Then the trouble began. One boy skied uncontrollable down a steep slope and disappeared over the edge. We were all dismayed. But before we reached the spot he had clambered out. A few more metres further on and he would have fallen a long way. In those days there were no cell phones so we would have been fairly helpless.

The route down was beginning to become very difficult. And then we came across a coloured pole indicating that we were indeed on the advanced route. We had lost our way, and could not return.

It was a hair-raising terrifying trip down. The slowing and stopping manoeuvres simply failed in icy snow, and we did not have the skills to cope. By the time we arrived at the bottom, still unable to slow down on the flat bridge covered in hail from the previous night, we were emotionally and physically exhausted. Cecil Scott commented, "That took more concentration than I had."

One fun thing for some of the macho boys was to have their photos taken standing in the snow whilst it was snowing wearing only their underpants. The strip off, photograph and rapid dressing only took a minute.

We travelled on to Italy. Wonderful sights. Sistine Chapel. St Peter's basilica. The museum or storage place with vast numbers of emasculated male nude statues.

We visited St Peter's twice. On the second occasion the Pope (John Paul II) was performing an ordination of some cardinals. The church was shut to the public, and a large number of Swiss Guards in colourful pantaloons and attire were on show.

We asked about going in to see and were refused.

What the Guards did not know was that a large side door (left from front) was left unlocked and very slightly ajar. A few of us slipped in unnoticed by the Swiss. The ceremony was in full flight and there was JP II walking down the aisle ahead of the presumably ordained or about to be ordained cardinals. We clambered across the chairs (everyone was standing) and we got an excellent close up view of his Holiness. I wanted to mention our escapade to the Swiss Guards, but one can never tell the outcome. I am not sure what the jails are like in Switzerland—probably quite civilized. Not like the overcrowded, over hot, often freezing, disease ridden, medication and doctor free, food and water deficient hell holes in Robert Mugabe's Zimbabwe.

Having seen the breath-taking beauty and magnificence of St Peter's, I could not help thinking that the so-called Great Zimbabwe Ruins was a pathetic and vastly inferior mess by comparison. Unfortunately the whole country could nowadays be aptly labelled the Zimbabwe Ruins.

On our last day in Rome some of us decided to avoid using the remains of our previous foreign exchange and try to hold out on purchasing any food. The hotel supplied a basic continental breakfast. Not much to fuel a busy day, but the occasional (or regular) fast does one's body and spirit the world of good.

We had a long and interesting day, slowly becoming more hungry. The kids, of course, had no concerns about spending their portion of the annual foreign exchange on food, but some of the staff knew they might need it for other out-of-country trips.

Time to get to the Rome airport.

When I saw the plane we were boarding my heart sank. It was full of dents all over the fuselage and engine cowlings. I wondered whether it had enough aerofoil capacity to lift off from the runway. The cockpit staff had already boarded, but the cabin staff were boarding just before we arrived. Not one of them was like the thin, sylphlike figures we had had on the journey out to Austria. My fear mounted as I imagined that with that amount of body mass on board without the passengers the plane had no hope of lift-off and would careen beyond the end of the runway only to crash in flames in the trees and buildings further on.

Of course the plane took off quite normally. But the food took an age to arrive. By the time it did the odour of our almost midnight dinner had us salivating to the point of drooling. We would have willingly consumed anything despite it being plane food.

I could see the lights from the Congo (as it was) below. A fair way from Rome. That part of Africa was at war. Is there any part of Africa that is not at war sometime? Wars and rumours of war appear to be a tradition on the African continent.

Two mouthfuls of food and suddenly the plane dropped out of the sky. I had visions of a ground to air rocket attack such as those two attacks on Air Rhodesia Viscounts returning to Salisbury from Kariba.

Our Air Zambia flight levelled out and carried on. It may have been an air pocket. Nevertheless it took me a while to feel like resuming my meal.

In the morning I asked one of the hostesses whether I could visit the pilot's cockpit. In those days it was common for passengers to visit the front of the plane and I almost always did. I spoke to the captain who was German and asked what happened in the night. His response astounded me. "Oh, ze autopilot failed. Often does."

And that was it.

FVH Why Cane Hard?

In England, my land of birth, where I have been living since 2005, the law forbade the smacking of a child by a parent let alone anyone else. A little bit of sense has prevailed since. Corporal punishment has long since been abolished in schools. Staff have been emasculated (or 'effemulated').

Combined with a general lack of parenting skills, and a confused moral compass, many young people have become unruly, uncontrollable, destructive, binge drinking alcoholics, and drug addicts. Many seem to be without direction, without hope.

In South Africa where I am also a citizen the new constitution which was instituted after years of apartheid has a very strong human rights component. The South African constitution is one of the best in the world. However, in order to accord human rights to children, corporal punishment in schools was outlawed. There was good reason for this because in many rural schools teachers used to beat the kids without mercy for the tiniest of infringements. This needed to be stopped.

However, the ban on all schools, no matter how good those schools are, and no matter how responsible the heads and the staff are, has been a steady decline in discipline and thus academic standards in all but the best state schools, and of course private schools where deviant kids can simply be expelled.

Yet both nations, Britain and South Africa, emanate from a strong Christian foundation which and both nations base many of their laws on the Bible, or at the very least moral biblical principles. Among the many wise concepts clearly stated in scripture is the need for the discipline of children using the rod of correction. Here are just a few clear statements from the Bible about such matters:

He who spares the rod hates his son, but he who loves him is careful to discipline him. [Proverbs 13: 24]

My son, do not despise the Lord's discipline and do not resent his rebuke, because the Lord disciplines those he loves, as a father the son he delights in. [Proverbs 3: 11-12]

Discipline your son, for in that there is hope; do not be a willing party to his death. [Proverbs 19: 18]

Folly is bound up in the heart of a child, but the rod of discipline will drive it far from him. [Proverbs 22: 15]

Do not withhold discipline from a child; if you punish him with the rod, he will not die. Punish him with the rod and save his soul from death. [Proverbs 23: 13-14]

The rod of correction imparts wisdom, but a child left to himself disgraces his mother. [Proverbs 29: 15]

Discipline your son, and he will give you peace; he will bring delight to your soul. [Proverbs 29: 17]

Endure hardship as discipline; God is treating you as sons. For what son is not disciplined by his father? If you are not disciplined (and everyone undergoes discipline), then you are illegitimate children and not true sons. [Hebrews 12: 7-8]

As a private tutor in England I would often give parents a printout of many Bible verses pertaining to strong loving discipline. Most were amazed, and most grateful for the enlightenment.

The boys at the schools where I taught were generally well behaved, polite and disciplined. It was when Bible principles were rejected or abandoned that society began to go wrong.

In the late seventies and early eighties in Rhodesia corporal punishment was part of normal school reality for boys. However, this was strictly regulated even to the point that government issue canes were the only ones to be used. There were strict limitations to how many 'strokes' could be administered to an individual in a day (six), and records were mandatory and the beatings record checked and signed by the head or deputy.

Housemasters and Superintendents were expected to administer corporal discipline.

I knew that many boys shrugged off a caning by walking out of the room facing their friends with a brave smile. However, they did not welcome the cane. I knew that although I did not like hurting youngsters I still needed to try to beat very hard and painfully. And never in anger because most of the cases were referred. On a very rare occasion, if I was angry. I would ask another member of staff to do my duty for me.

As a large man and, in those days quite strong, I put all my effort into a beating. (I learned later from former pupils, now friends, I was quite feeble at caning. If true, good.)

A regular caning usually only required two 'strokes'; anything more was for really serious offenses. Smoking and drinking brought about six.

I do not recall any boy crying out, or even crying. They were a brave lot and knew their friends were just outside the door. Boys were never beaten unless they deserved it.

The reader may think this all rather sadistic, so to answer the question, "Why cane hard?" It was to keep those boys away from further trouble. Self discipline would soon become part of their lives. Sometimes the threat of punishment is a strong deterrent. Furthermore they had something to tell their children and grandchildren. "When I was a boy . . ."

So that you do not think me heartless, I got one of the staff to beat me as they would a boy so I knew what it felt like. Not pleasant. But it was not meant to be.

Occasionally a boy would stuff an exercise book or two into his pants. It would make a thwack sound totally different from the norm. One had to appear stern and very seriously angry at this attempt to avoid pain, but it took me a great deal of self-control not to laugh out loud at the audacity.

Many years later at a Fort Victoria High School reunion in the mid-nineties I was greeted warmly by many of those young men whom I had beaten, and amidst handshakes offered beers. Never any hard feelings either in hostel or later.

Looking back on memories it seems that, in the main, the majority of boys only ever got one or two beatings in their entire school career, and some were never beaten because they were either crafty, or naturally law abiding, or both.

That is as it should be.

FVH Beatings at Tower House

When I first took over Tower House I spent a month working on the paperwork left over by my predecessor who had departed rather precipitously. I rarely went to bed before 3am during that time. I performed all necessary duties as superintendent—mealtimes, prefect meetings, inspections when I was on duty and conferences with the three matrons. And of course teaching and sports duties and running the science department. Other than that I focussed on getting all the paperwork straight and was a little distant in that I only appeared in the hostel when necessary.

This led to the boys treating me with a little awe as they did not know who or what I was. I was a distant entity. They were wary of 'The Superintendent' and I knew it. I had to rely on my inherited untried prefects and hostel staff to keep order until I was able to emerge from dark into light. I am reporting the facts, as I remember them. I am nothing special in myself.

One of the documents I found quite early in my clean up was the beatings record book. All canings had to be done using an official government standard cane—not too thin and flexible for fear of a wrap around and damage to genitals, no more than six strokes of the cane were allowed on any one day, and the incident had to be recorded citing reason and the number of strokes given. Only the boys could be beaten. The girls had to do manual tasks such as weeding. Many girls longed for and regularly requested a beating, over within minutes not the long hours in the sun. Beating girls was against the law. Prefects, including the Head Boy, were not allowed to cane any boy.

As I studied that beatings record book I felt immense increasing compassion for those poor boys. (I never cry in public. But I wept for those kids in private.) I knew some of them from my science classes. I had observed many of them during my brief encounters in the hostel. They were most certainly not evil or bad kids. And never would be. Most of them were brought up in an Afrikaans environment. This meant (most often) a loving home, good food, sensible discipline and Christian values. Most of those boys would never have needed corporal punishment under an intelligent humane regime. They could easily have transported or transcended themselves through their high school career without having been caned once. I have friends, former tutees and pupils, and many second cousins who might agree.

I still believe in the Biblical injunction that sparing the rod will spoil the child, and that a father who does not discipline his son hates his son. (As superintendent I was *in loco parentis*).

The nonsense over human rights in England has led to yobbish behaviour, anti-socialism, disrespect for authority including older people and parents, widespread substance abuse (cigarettes, alcohol and worse) reduced teacher authority and classroom control, inefficient use of lesson time, general ignorance, falling standards, dumbed down exams and worst of all breathtaking illiteracy despite 12 years of schooling. Many British people fear the youth, despite the fact that there are many wonderful young people. I know several from my church, and have a large number of second and third cousins who are very good sorts. Sheer stupidity in my view on the part of Parliament, and essentially anti-Christian, anti-Muslim, and anti many other morally based religions has led to this.

I therefore determined that for Tower House I would reduce the number of beatings to the absolutely necessary minimum. I realized that the plethora of petty rules within the hostel made it almost impossible for any young lad to avoid breaking one or more rules during the course of a day. It was mere good (possibly Angelic) fortune if they avoided detection. Tower House had become an unhappy prison. Good intentions, much like government, often end up badly when God is not obeyed or Jesus considered. Suffer the little children to come unto me. Big 'children' also need love. Lots of it.

Having analysed all the rules I decided to scrap almost all of the rules in favour of two areas of operation.

The first was to do with routine efficient functioning of the hostel. Roll calls, meal times, prep times, dorm and clothing inspections, lights out times.

The second had to do with ethics, morality, respectful behaviour to everyone—staff, matrons, prefects and of course each other. Honesty and truth was to be valued above the multitude of fibs and lies to which cornered boys had to resort in order to avoid pain and suffering. I wanted to remove any need or temptation to be dishonest.

I held a council with the four prefects and the four sub-prefects. We discussed every aspect of hostel policy and management. There appeared to be some relief among the eight prefect team at my proposals. [I not remember whether I plied them with sweet Marsala wine, but I may have done. *In vino veritas.*]

They realized that they would, if they accepted the scheme, no longer be the demons of the dormitories, feared and hated. Some had younger brothers in Tower House and their prefect position put pressure on their siblings. They sensed that perhaps they would gain back the confidence of their own brothers, and perhaps the earned respect of many other 'brothers'. The key elements were to be love and mercy tempered with justice and fair play.

The changes were unanimously accepted and adopted by the prefect group of eight.

The next task was to inform the rest of the hostel. This needed to be done carefully, tactfully, sensibly. The boys should be clear that misbehaviour in terms of higher order moral and ethical issues would be dealt with firmly. No form of bullying, physical, emotional or psychological would be countenanced (not the actual word I used, but the concept carefully explained). Those boys needed to feel safe. The staff, including teaching staff, matrons, ground and cleaning staff (mostly black) and the prefects were to be treated politely and with respect. Thus the authority of the prefects was established within a framework which transcended multiple sets of pointless rules.

The boys were told about the abolishment of all petty rules. Moral ethical principles would be applied instead. All hostel dwellers were not only to feel free but have freedom along with responsibility. They needed to be well turned out for school. Clean shoes, tidy, hair combed and clean and fresh in body. Operational rules were explained in terms of the general good of all. Be on time for morning roll call at second bell. But come as you are. You may have just woken up (adolescent boys need more sleep than their younger brothers—a now proven and established phenomenon) and there would be time to dress for school after breakfast. A towel, a dressing gown, a sheet— but do turn up on time to check in. For your own and other's security.

The most important principle which took a little time to sink in was that anyone who was forwarded for caning would have the right of appeal. This meant that any boy who felt unfairly accused would be able to state his own case. It was easy to spot the frauds. The relevant dormitory prefect was brought in on the discussion. In many cases the prefect agreed to issue a warning. Usually the grateful boys did not repeat the usually minor misdemeanours. Those who needed corporal punishment received it. I tended to be an advocate for the youngster regarding a bum beating using reason and sense. I took no happiness in hitting young boys with a cane. I tended to weep alone after such necessary canings.

It was especially important to me that I avoided caning a boy who was older than about fourteen. The age of reason. Suffer the children who come unto me said The Lord Jesus.

Any young man in the hostel had the right to report to his prefect or to me any incidence of any form or kind of bullying from anyone, however minor or unperceived. It would be investigated.

I instituted four major reforms.

We had a number of ex-patriot staff (German, Australian etc.) who tended to take advantage of the cheap alcohol prices in the country by arriving inebriated for hostel duty. I gave the prefects the full powers to physically restrain such staff, and take over, in order to protect their wards, and it was to be upon my authority. I would take the consequences, not them. I banned one Australian teacher from Tower House because he was pushing marijuana. The headmaster—Barry Maytham, a good man—took strong action with the local ministry of education to ensure that this reprobate was removed from his post. Rapidly. Barry was a man of action and a very good headmaster. The Australian ex pat was thus evicted from his post. In another section I tell the tale of Barry's very good influence on the school.

We did not need such so-called teachers, drug pushers, in the hostel.

In winter the main male sport was rugby. The ladies played hockey. Mostly coached by the deputy head, Roy McRindle. Rugby practice took more time for the first and second and older senior teams than for the junior teams. The junior teams got back to the hostel earlier and bathed and showered first. The hot water ran out before the older gentlemen returned. The older guys were dirty, smelly, tired and really needed a hot bath or shower before supper. But the water was always cold. It would be winter in rugby season. Africa can be very cold in winter in the evenings when the sun has retired.

Tower was the oldest hostel and the water heating system would never keep up with 72 boys in four dormitories. Neither would it have kept up in winter in any of the other four hostels. But the school rule was that the boys must only use their own bathrooms, and only at specific times. The hot water tank was only one or a set, fairly large volume serving all four dormitories, but only one main source hot water source for the entire four dorms.

I understood the frustration, anger and resentment of the older boys towards the juniors. They had a point, and a case. Who would want to arrive for a cleansing soothing warm wash, after heavy physical work, to cold water? But the situation was a potential powder keg of resentment.

The solution was elegant, simple, imparted more freedom and inspired greater responsibility and, I admit, God inspired. I announced that all boys could take a bath or shower in any of the four dormitories below them. This meant that the privacy of the more senior dorms could not be infringed by the dorms below them. The most junior dorm could only wash in their junior dorm bathroom. Seniors could use any of the four bathrooms. Any time of the day with procedural exceptions. Result? Cleaner and happier youngsters and young men. Much less smellier. Much happier hostel matrons. The Lord was kind and merciful to those loveable people.

I threatened that any more senior boy who bullied a less junior boy who may be showering would be caned and permanently banned from entering that dormitory. Any boy, no matter how junior, in a bath or shower had to be allowed to finish his washing. Non interference. No bullying. And, of course, the right of appeal was in place. Those who wanted to dare did not dare to dare. The prefects had to keep a watchful eye on this, and they did.

This 'bath time' coup de grace was revolutionary in terms of the school's general rules and procedures and I had to solemnly warn the entire Tower House contingent i.e. all staff (especially the three matrons) and kids to keep the plot strictly confidential. If this leaked out to the rest of the school we would be compelled to return to the previous system of cold water for the First and Second Teams. I suspect everyone was excited and motivated by the conspiracy.

The next stage towards newer freedom was that any boy could shower or bath in their own dorm or lower at any time of the day, morning, lunchtime or evening as long as it did not disturb anyone else or cut across scheduled prep times. Hot water for all whenever they needed it. Morning, after school, evening, whenever. Two baths or showers per day in the hot sweaty summers if necessary. Just do not inconvenience the sleep of others at night. The electricity bill had to have increased. But who cared? I didn't. As an old university friend, Reverend Dr Bryden Black, once said, "People are more important than things." I agreed. People need love and care and compassion.

The side effects were unpredicted. Happier young men were predicted. More hot water was predicted. Higher electricity bills was predicted.

But the improved relationships between younger boys seeing their senior counterparts naked in their bathrooms gave them a sense of liberty to talk to and gain advice and friendship from those older boys in the hostel and at school. There was never an issue over the bathrooms again whilst I was *'episcopos'* [Latin name for Bishop]. Happiness increased.

I give credit and glory and fully to the help ideas from a Divine Higher Power. He who loves me still despite my manifold faults and failings. He gave me undeserved Wisdom. I grew to love those people in my care. He loves them infinitely more than I.

FVH Afternoon Prep Changes in Tower House

Rhodesia (now Zimbabwe) is quite a warm place, and Fort Victoria (now Masvingo) is quite soporific in the afternoons, especially in summer.

The school hostel routine was that after school and after luncheon the pupils would sit down sleepily in the sultry heat of the afternoon for an hour or so of prep before afternoon sport activities. 'Keep them busy and out of mischief.' (I mention elsewhere that boys need to get into mischief as long as it is not evil.)

I noticed that many of the younger boys did not have enough to do regarding homework and were quite bored and probably (I never asked) frustrated with this arrangement. They simply sat after lunch time and endured the hour. My heart went out to them. Some were part of the ESN (Educationally Sub-Normal—differently gifted is the politically correct euphemism) group and could not have done homework anyway. My teacher training at the (then brilliant) University of Rhodesia had taught me a few things about education and kids. Friends in education taught me a few other things (such as the fact that adolescent boys need more sleep than their younger counterparts).

At our weekly 'fireside chat' (no actual fire—just a term from a former American president on his weekly radio broadcasts before the ubiquitous TV) on my Monday duty day after lunching I took the chaps into my confidence and proposed a scheme which might make them happier. It had to be agreed upon by all. It had to be kept a complete secret from the rest of the school.

The proposal was that afternoon prep was to become voluntary. The agreement had to have several conditions. Nobody was to leave the hostel during that afternoon prep period. Any boy wandering around during afternoon prep time would blow the whole scheme. Everyone had to be totally quiet. Bathing was allowed, but in silence. Anyone not downstairs doing prep should be in their dorms doing what they wanted—reading, sleeping, homework, whatever. I think the boys were excited about the plan and just as excited at keeping the secret.

The whole hostel agreed, and I knew I could trust them. They were good people, and there must have been a certain loyalty between them. In any case the older young men would have made sure that the possibly wayward juniors, who might have blown the plan, would tow the party line.

The scheme was implemented. I had to inform my supervising hostel staff and the matrons. A risk. They too kept the secret. They also wanted the happiness of kids away from family.

I also wanted to cover myself. Every term there were test and exam records written (by hand—no word processors in those days) for every form class. I got the records for all my boys and recording them privately in my own log. I did this for five school terms. There were three terms per year.

And after nearly two years of running this afternoon free prep scheme the imperious Ma Scott confronted me. "I hear, Mr Stone, that your hostel does not do afternoon prep!" I said yes, even though it was only partially true as the older boys had more prep than the juniors (not diplomatic to argue that point at that time), but I also reported that every boy's marks had improved. That was actually true. I had the evidence. How could Ma Scott answer that?

Happiness breeds more enthusiasm. Sometimes less is more. Letting kids take some responsibility for their own learning is better that dictatorial authoritarianism.

FVH Contrasting Prime Ministers

On two occasions the Hostel kids were allowed to be up past their bedtime over midnight to hear the opening speech of two new prime ministers. Ian Smith was ousted. The first prime minister was the recently deceased Bishop Abel Muzorewa. He was a Methodist minister and a good man. Under his leadership the country ran well.

His opening line, at midnight as the country became Zimbwbe-Rhodesia with Muzorewa as head of government, on the radio was a quote from the Psalms.

"This is the day that the Lord has made. Let us be glad, very glad (slight deviation from the scripture)".

For the first year of the new Zimbabwe-Rhodesia things were good under Abel. I will meet him in The Kingdom. The new constitution allowed the whites a certain amount of veto power (28 votes) over constitutional change.

Ironically the white Members of Parliament wanted the good of the country and the welfare of the black people just as much as the black MPs. As far as I remember not a single proposed parliamentary bill was opposed. They were all sensible and good. Life under the Bishop was good.

But the new government was an internally sorted government. Robert Gabriel Mugabe had been side-lined. R G Mugabe had (it was rumoured) decided to give up his bush warfare.

I have two complaints about Margaret Thatcher, arguably one of the best British Prime Ministers apart from Churchill in centuries. The second complaint is that she apparently scuppered plans to have a railway constructed within the M25—a really sensible plan considering transport costs and city congestion these days.

The first complaint about Thatcher is that as a new Prime Minister she and Ronald Reagan plotted to have a conference at Lancaster House with Rhodesian, Zimbabwe-Rhodesian and guerrilla leaders. I was compelled to be a police reservist at the good Muzorewa election and one year later the sinister evil Mugabe stolen election. Thirty some years on, years of ongoing unfair incarcerations, torture, suffering and death, R G M in his psychotic paranoiac dictatorship aged 90 something has ruined a perfectly good country.

I own a photograph in South Africa which I took in 1980 of a small chap called Glen Stephens. I mentioned this previously. He is now dead from an illness he had. I will meet him again in Heaven. He is pictured standing in a crater made by a bomb designed to destroy Mugabe who was on the election campaign trail and on the way to the local airport. The bomb exploded one second too late. Regrettably. Thirty years of misery may have ensued.

One second earlier may have allowed Zimbabwe a survival opportunity. Instead the people, my compatriots, suffer whilst the dictator accumulates wealth to the tune of millions, and hijacks Air Zimbabwe planes in order to do shopping in the Far East with his entourage (quislings with zero moral sense) using money that should have gone to the people of Zimbabwe.

Mugabe's radio speech, which I thought the Tower House gentlemen should hear as an historic event, began totally in contrast to the Bishop.

"Revolutionary greetings in the name of freedom."

That was the beginning of an age of terror.

FVH Mischief and Fun

One advantage of being a superintendent was reduced sporting responsibilities. The five superintendents had more than enough to do in the week running the hostels. So it was considered only fair to let us 'babysit' the sports teams (as such) with least potential. They would never need to travel to compete, so escorting them was unnecessary. Stress reduction for all of us was most welcome.

And so it was that I supervised a bunch of boys who had no clue about cricket. Practices (never leading to anything) were an absolute riotous scream. They could not hit a ball. They could not catch a ball. They could not bowl a ball. They could not hit a wicket. They had little danger of ever being promoted to higher levels and having to endure weekend trips to other schools for matches. Perhaps they planned it that way, and deliberately played badly. [I once pretended—as a schoolboy limey in Rhodesia—not to be able to swim. I did not want to use up my Saturdays going to inter-school swimming galas. So, being a very adept swimmer—we had a pool at home and regularly used the local swimming baths in England—I did doggy paddle in the shallow end whilst my compatriots exhausted themselves swimming fast lengths of the main pool. I just asked the question: "What do you do if you cannot swim?" Everything else was assumed.]

Besides all that—going back to Fort Victoria High, cricket is quite a drag for some people.

But we all had many laughs, and at least the lads were outside in the sunshine and fresh air getting some exercise.

One funniest moment for us was when a chap threw, not bowled, a ball so high and wide, and so impossible to reach, that as ball flew past the batsman his creative solution was to throw his bat into to air in an effort to connect with that horrendous wide.

We fell about in great mirth.
. . . .

A young soccer player had the odd first name of Christmas. I never asked him why. Many black people have such sort of names, and they usually signify something. Perhaps he was born on Christmas day.

In an effort to be nice to the kids I would ask them about their aspirations. Christmas told me he wanted to become a Catholic Priest.

It took a little time to realise he was having me on. He would have been called Father Christmas.

. . . .

On a late evening routine hostel checking round I accidentally came across two young men trying to bunk out. I must have looked a little dumbfounded. The one lad said something like, "Oh sir. I do wish you had not caught us." They were both two un-wicked good kids and both in the ESN class. A touch of mischief. A touch of fun. Trying not to show it, my heart melted at that plea. I was stern in voice about them needing to get back to bed. They obeyed. Who would not love such an open admission of guilt?

I had to laugh and did nothing further. They went to bed without punishment. I blessed them both.

. . . .

In Fort House we had many very effective prefects. I will mention one (and for his sake) will call him P. Being a good prefect he needed to conceal a vice. He smoked, and only when he was about to leave school did he tell me about it. Smoking was illegal and not acceptable for a schoolboy. He concealed his addiction with craft and aplomb. I was usually good at 'smoking detection.'

I think of him as brave young person who trusted me enough to keep his secret.

He was also a hot blooded tall, muscular, good looking male with much enthusiastic popularity with the ladies. He was definitely sexy. They fell over themselves to have a dance with him at the school dance events.

And then I saw him placing a two golf balls into his pocket before such a dance event. So I asked him why the golf balls.

So in fun P, near the end of his school days, suddenly pulled me and hugged me (his housemaster!) to himself.

I was quite alarmed. He was very strong. "What do you feel?" he asked. I did not answer. I actually knew he wanted to arouse the dance girls with what they would have thought was a large penile erection on his part.

I remain highly amused to this day.

FVH *The Oil Storage Tanks*

It was school holiday call-up and military stand by. Val Mogg suggested we stay in his grandmother's place as we were both likely to be summonsed and I had no easy to hear telephone. Pity that. I should have stayed in the hostel and thus avoid a call-out. The authorities could have collected me, but not easily through the fences and locked security gates.

The allure of wine and whiskey and Val's good cooking had me over at Gran's. She was away. So one late evening whilst watching television a huge nearby explosion occurred. We both ran out of the house. A vast mushroom plume of fire was ascending over by the large oil storage drums about two miles away. We felt the radiant heat from the fire where we stood. There were houses very close by to those oil tanks.

I feared greatly for the life of a family, the Pingstone's, living just opposite, friends and colleagues from the school. They were unhurt. The heat and smoke travelled upwards, away from the houses. I was greatly relieved. They were good people.

'Frodo' Mogg and I got into our military uniform. And waited. And waited some more.

Two hours later, near to midnight we received the phone call. Come immediately to the police station was the demand. What a crowd of slow coaches. Two hours?

We both knew it was about to happen. But two hours later?

Then another wasted hour whilst the slowly creeping cops decided that we needed to patrol down the stream which ran past the oil tanks, and towards the black township where it was assumed the attackers would have taken cover. Stupid useless military. The attackers were very long gone three hours earlier. Or so we hoped. It would be have been easy to ambush a patrol under cover of darkness.

We were transported to the oil storage drums which had now burned out. Thus began the patrol. I had a radio for the team on my side of the stream, and Val Mogg had the radio for his team on the other side of the river.

I had my radio on 'squelch' meaning that the signal was not as strong, but the radio was free from hiss and crackle. Val did not switch his radio to squelch, so one could hear the continuous hissing across the stream throughout the entire trip.

My team moved with stealth through the tall grass, not speaking to each other at all. Val's team crashed their way through with Val constantly cursing and swearing.

It is an evil thought as I remember back because I realized that if anyone was to be hit first by any ambush it would be his side. Shame on me.

In any event, as predicted, we found nothing. And were grateful.

It is a wonder that technically, and once the Muzorewa elections had taken place.

FVH Removing Porn in the Dorm

The boys of Tower House almost all came from good moral homes. Many were Christian. But the older boys had been seduced into believing that they needed a picture or two of nude women in their work spaces. It was most probably due to peer pressure. If they were not imagined to be hot blooded sexually mature males they would be suspected of being homosexual. (Gay is just about the most useless term for people who cannot help their sexual preference. Most are not gay in the old sense of the word. They are often quite unhappy, alcoholic and suicidal. I knew a few who were in such a predicament. The church view is that they should be loved for themselves, but not their actions. After all, what heterosexual man has not lusted after the flesh of women who they have mentally undressed? Same problem.)

The senior boys with pornography would also probably be embarrassed if any of their family or older friends saw their decor. They did not really want it.

I had decided that this was not an acceptable thing. Younger boys often entered the work areas of the older boys and would be subjected to the scenes of female nudity. Not good. Degrading to women and to boys. Most would be happily married one day. (I am in email contact with such happily married former hostel dwellers.) Mental images of women with large breasts would not have helped with their future love life.

I assembled the prefects and sub-prefects for a discussion in my flat. The conversation was all to do with pornography in the hostel. I was very direct, and knew some of them may have felt quite shy about such conversation. They knew I was serious.

Wonderfully, to a man, they unanimously agreed that the porn should be purged. I was impressed with their integrity and maturity. Consensus. The prefects themselves had the pictures removed. It was probably a great relief to most of the young men.

What the prefects did not know, and were never told, was if they had not complied with my attitude I would have acted unilaterally and ordered the removal of the pornography anyway.

It is sometimes better to have support for a good cause by the leaders.

FVH Sugar

One dimension of colonial school life was tea.

As Superintendent a tray with teacup, teapot, sugar bowl and milk jug would be on my office desk at 6-30 am. Two cups of tea in the flat whilst getting dressed and ready for roll call.

There was tea in the staff room at first break. Usually two cups.

Tea at lunch time in the dining area. Two more cups.

Afternoon tea after prep and before sport and other activities.

More tea during the evening meal.

Tea served at around about 8pm.

One always drank at least one cup but usually two. The Lowveld is a very warm place.

I took tea with milk and two teaspoons of sugar in those days.

One lunchtime, when the kids were changing for sport and getting ready for afternoon prep I took an unused teacup and spooned in the number of spoons of sugar per tea event. Four before, breakfast, four at school break and so on . . . .

By the end of the day the sugar cup was full to overflowing. I was shocked. That amount of sugar was dangerously excessive.

I decided there and then to give up sugar in tea.

It was strange and a little hard to begin with. But I persevered, and now do not like sugar in tea—an occasional mistake by a host. Teas of all kinds taste much better without sugar.

Since that day in 1981 I have learned that sugar suppresses the body's immune system.

Dr Nancy Appleton compiled a vast amount of research into a well referenced book entitled 'Lick the Sugar Habit' [76 Ways Sugar Can Ruin Your Health]. Every parent should get hold of that book. I usually gave a summary to the parents of my tutees when I noticed that sugar, in various forms, was a large part of their diet.

The greatest cause of death in youngsters in America is not obesity (few young people die of obesity). Neither is it diabetes (which is manageable and can be controlled).

It is cancer. Ironically cancer is easily preventable by a good anti-oxidant diet and many forms of cancer can be controlled to permanent remission with the right foods. That coupled with a good immune system can avoid cause the avoidance of most cancers and sometimes cure certain kinds of cancers.

Sugar certainly does not help.

FVH Stand up be good for Photos

Although I loved the boys of Tower House I knew I needed to help them in responsibility and dignity and respect. No weakness on my part. People need self esteem. Young men are no different.

One of the failures of British society is that many parents cannot parent their kids, and teachers have had almost all their powers stripped away. Only about five percent of British people attend church, and some of those may never have had a life-changing encounter with Jesus Christ.

I informed the young gentlemen that when I, the superintendent, approached the hostel, they must stand up in respect of my station and position. So each time I returned from school those nice kids, junior and senior, stood up. I am still proud of them. And I would never whack them for not being upstanding. They never knew that, although I suspect that some of the prefects knew I would never punish small boys for such a trivial matter. If they knew anything at all it was part of the game. I was really thinking of them, and could really not care less about me.

Annually there would be the school photographs. Hostel photos were part of that. Again, I was proud of my wards and wanted them to stand for the photos with pride and dignity.

We had a dear old man from town who had taken the school photos for years. He was a no nonsense fellow, much respected, and a great help when I threatened my team of good guys that should they mess about with faces in the photo it would show up in the picture and I would thrash them with the cane. I never would have done so. Boys must be boys. I messed with photographs myself. But I was mindful of the material costs to that old man.

I also made the standing photo arrangement even. Tall to short, large to small, seniors at the back and descending year groups to the most junior at the front. Pretty routine. Those photos were good. Well planned and holding some good memories, I hope.

A credit to the old man.

FVH Federick Naudé

One of the best prefects in Tower House was Fred Naudé.

He was a strapping lad, tall and strong. First Team rugby captain. I knew the family. Had a delicious luncheon of local game one time at their farm.

Fred was in charge of the hostel. It was quite a responsibility. He had a lover in the form of a local American minister's daughter called Mary. I always knew of his liaisons with his lifelong sweetheart, but as a man of the world I let events take their course. Fred sometimes illegally slipped out of the hostel for a bit of fellowship with Mary and her wonderful family. There would be no sex. I knew that much. Christian upbringing and watchful dad. And Frederick was an honourable good Afrikaans Christian young man. He married that girlfriend after he had left school, and the last time I had any news of them they were living in America. I did not apply the letter of the law. Legalism kills the human spirit. What is needed is an understanding of the spirit of the law tempered with some good common sense.

The hostel can be a bit of a prison, hence regulations to protect the boys. Fred needed protection. Besides, the pastor's house was a couple of blocks away in that small town, and Fred always did his duties well. Why not do a little bunking from time to time? In those days prefects had precious few 'privileges'.

One of the hostel rules I imposed on the fantastic hostel prefects was that they should always report to me any incidents which they may have incurred. In other words should they have incurred a difficulty with their wards they needed (for their own protection) to come to me in the superintendent's flat and report any incident immediately. Before the 'victim' came to complain. It was for the protection of the prefects in the event of a complaint or inquiry.

Knowing the frailty and fragility of human beings (self included) it was inevitable that prefects would become totally frustrated with some of their juniors. Boys can be naughty. Mischief was fine, but bad behaviour was not fine. Youngsters, like adults, can be extremely manipulative. The job of prefects was quite tough at times.

I do not remember the actual incident but Fred under severe provocation from a junior boy perhaps had given him a much deserved slap. I was impressed by his restraint. I might have given a good hiding. Or kicking.

Fred arrived at my office within minutes of the incident looking dreadful. Sensing the situation I invited him out of the office, lest we were disturbed, through to the superintendent's lounge which was off the office.

He started to cry with uncontrollable sobs. He confessed that he had hurt one of the boys who really deserved punishment. I wanted to console this big young man with a hug but thought better of it at that point. Instead I consoled this weeping prefect with an assurance that he had justly dealt with the indigent and no comeback would happen on his part. Besides, he had come directly to me immediately—a sign of responsibility. A much relieved man wiped his eyes, got himself together, before I summonsed the offending youngster.

I gave the boy who had caused the trouble a bit of a difficult time. Firm words and a strong reprimand How dare he be rude to his superior? Especially Frederick, the head prefect of hostel. What reason or reasons did he have for his rude behaviour? What would his parents think? Should I write them a letter? The offending boy knew he was in the wrong and apologized to the Head of House. He was let off with a stern warning. I was not about to cane him. Rational discussion is almost always better than violence.

I think Fred was happy with the outcome, and felt more secure in his position. He never slapped another boy as far as I know.

The fascinating thing was that after that I do not recall any other prefect needing to come to report.

Perhaps word got around: Don't mess with the prefects. Stone was not going to consider complaints which were semi-fabricated.

FVH Morning Time Routine

A scheduled morning routine was pre breakfast roll call. It was done for the safety of the kids. If anyone was missing or had bunked out or was ill we needed to know.

I noticed that quite often when I was running late and struggling to get to morning roll call so were the boys. On some nights we all slept a little longer.

It was a little like those women institutes where menstruation seemed to synchronize.

Solution? Stop fussing, within a reasonable and practical time frame, about being exactly on time for roll call. There would be time for breakfast. So a few minutes lateness was part of the flexibility, as long as the boys got there in reasonable time, and as long as they arrived.

So I unofficially had morning roll attached to superintendent's arrival. The prefects knew this of course. I had no desire to punish any boy for being a couple of minutes late because of night time weather conditions. In winter we all slept more soundly.

As far as I know (and I do not know) no hostel dweller took advantage of this small temporal flexibility.

FVH Mother did not recognise Son

A hilarious event happened one afternoon. One of the younger boys wanted to phone home. So he came to the office and rang. He appeared to have got through.

"It's Paul," Then again, "Paul!" Puzzled expression on face. "Your son!" Relief. Mother had worked it out.

FVH Curtains and Beds

When I first started as superintendent of Tower House, the oldest hostel, I noticed that the bedding was old, the curtains drab, and I thought the boys deserved better. I put a scheme into action, knowing that if the local Education Department were asked directly for new curtains and bedding they would, pleading lack of funds, say, 'No!'

However, a certain teacher called Bill Pingstone had been with the school for years, and was known to be a man of honour and integrity. It was his house and family I feared for when the oil storage tanks were rocketed.

Bill Pingstone, a truly nice kind man, was in charge of authorising what was know as 'boarding'. This meant getting rid of the old and moving into the new. But it had to be official. I asked Bill to look at the disgrace of tatty beige curtains, hard beds, and ancient bedspreads. Tower House was the first hostel built when the school was started, and those aforementioned items would most likely have been there for more than twenty years.

Bill agreed, and signed off the curtains etc. as 'boarded' i.e. to be disposed of.

From the government suppliers I ordered new nice colourful curtains. I ordered new mattresses for the beds. I ordered new bedspreads. Amazingly they all arrived. The old stuff got taken away; the new goods installed. It transformed the place from something that looked like a prison to something that looked a bit like a home.

A few weeks later I was served with a letter of reprimand from the Ministry. They were very dismayed, annoyed and angry that I had dared to spend 'their' money on what was considered unnecessary items. I do not remember writing a contrite letter of apology, but I may have. One must be diplomatic in such matters I think.

Ask me if I cared about the reprimand. My boys were my main concern and I loved them. It was bad enough having to live in a hostel hundreds of miles—in some case—from home. I would like to believe the new decor and the more comfortable beds made them happier.

There is an old, but sensible, adage: It is easier to obtain forgiveness than permission.

FVH *The Day Luncheon Bully*

At a particular time one year a day pupil was allowed to lunch in Tower House. Only to lunch and prep. His parents were both working and they wanted to see him supervised and fed.

Within a few days it became apparent that he was bullying the younger boys. I cannot recall how I came upon this information, but I remember checking it out. It appeared to be true. I was incensed and had become protective of 'my boys'.

After questioning the alleged bully I realized that he was a potential threat to the happiness and well being of the younger boys. He would never have dared try to bully a contemporary or anyone above.

When I was at Junior school in Heston in the 1960's we had a bully. He mostly bullied the girls. The week before the end of school, and the time we seniors would leave, there was a leaver's party and a magic show for us after the food. Between the meal and the show we all went out onto the fields whilst the hall was cleared and seats put in for the performance. Whilst seated in the grass with some friends a cluster of girls came up to us crying. The bully had bullied them again. We and they were angry so we got up and marched menacingly toward him. He saw us and started to run away. We chased him around the fields and very soon the entire final year pupil body were chasing him. He was a bit of a fatty, but I have never seen such a fat boy run so fast. He escaped by running into the hall where the teachers were. There he stayed until the end of the show. Justice at last.

In order to prevent further bullying incidents in Tower House, and in order to ensure that the young boys knew they would be protected I informed the prefects. They were equally protective of their own Tower House 'brothers'. We came to an agreement.

I changed the seating arrangement for meals and made the bully sit alone on his own table away from everyone else in the dining room. It was a good example for the youngsters, and others. Righteousness had prevailed. Good had won over evil.

The bully was suitably 'bullied' back by being humiliated. After about a week of this he stopped coming to lunch time meals. Halleluiah.

Strangely, I do not recall seeing him in the school. Perhaps he was steering clear of me.

FVH Drinks in The Flat

From time to time I invited the prefects for an after supper glass of Marsala wine in the Superintendent's flat. We never overdid the alcohol, but it was a congenial event and allowed me to discern any difficulties with duties. They were, after two glasses of sweet Marsala wine—about 15%—a little more relaxed and a little more garrulous. These were good times of fellowship, and learned much about hostel goings on which I would never, otherwise, have known.

On one occasion there was knock at the front door. Nobody usually came in the front door as the hostel was always open so access to the superintendent generally happened through the office. In trepidation I went to open it.

It turned out to be the headmaster, the strict disciplinarian Barry Maytham. He was dressed as though he was going out. I cannot recall the reason for the visit, but he clearly saw that we chaps were sitting around boozing. But I suppose in those days laws and rules of school were not quite as restrictive as they are today. We could have a bit of fun and a laugh with the students. Besides, those after dinner drinks made us feel more like a family.

You may wonder whether their parents would approve. The fact was that those boys were drinking beer on the farm since they became teenagers. Drinking was part of the social scene where entertainment was sparse on the farms.

Barry stated his business—I have no recollection of what it was about. Then he left. Nothing else was said. Ever. It was as if it never happened.

FVH Renovation and Paint

Tower House needed a thorough paint job and a little more care and attention than it was getting. When I took over Tower the place was painted out in boring government colours. Mainly greys and dull green. And rather tatty. No wonder some of the boys thought it was like a prison.

I wrote rather persuasively with a hint of emotion and a good dose of feigned alarm to the local works department. Basically I stated that the hostel was crumbling away, and wondered who would be to blame, and saying that if someone did not sort out this government building quite quickly it might be too late.

For some mysterious reason they believed me, or needed the work, and spent six months painting everything from roof through to the whole outside to all of the inside. Every crack sealed, every hole filled. All woodwork re-glossed.

After their six month effort a few things needed a repaint. This was done willingly. Although it took some time, at the end of it all the place looked modern, refreshed, cared for.

I was consulted on dormitory colours. I knew about the calming peaceful effects of light green and light blue. So the three most junior dorms were painted out in those nice sensibly light and bright colours.

Wickedly I asked that the senior dormitory to be painted out in a light pink. I was being sarcastic (although I am sure few, if any recognised that) and thought that lady pink might have brought the older lads down a step or two. Older lads can become a fraction arrogant. Strangely I received an email from one of the former 'inmates' which was addressed to a contemporary of his in the hostel. For quite a few months now we have been sharing emails between the three of us.

That particular email mentioned the colour of the senior dormitory and suggested that it was a colour to calm and sooth the seniors.

I do not think this ruse and misplaced joke worked and have since regretted my sinful evil decision. I should have asked for a calming light green. I need forgiveness for that.

FVH Late Homework Workers

There were a small few conscientious pupils in Tower House who often worked late into the evening. This concerned me as I knew they needed their sleep and working when tired is not efficient. Working until after 11 pm and having to be up and about from 6-30 am would not have given them enough good sleep. If there was school the next day they would have been too tired to concentrate. As mentioned elsewhere adolescent boys need more sleep than their younger non-teenage sibling.

In later communications with a couple of those lads they (as husbands and fathers) confessed that they did not always do homework, but took the opportunity of a quiet place with most of the other boys in bed to indulge in some deep and meaningful conversations, and some not so meaningful or deep. One can hardly blame them. Hostel life is not especially private, and despite being in the country few wanted to wander alone too far into the surrounding bush.

The plot I conceived was to invite them for tea and possibly biscuits. It meant they would stop slaving away and would finally go to bed. And then I could rest and go to bed in relative peace.

The plan was simple. I would wander out through the office off the foyer, check the front doors, then check the windows in the dining cum prep area where they were seated 'working', then check the back door next to the back stairs. And then decide to notice them, and suggest they needed a pre-bed cup of tea and biscuits.

They always took up this offer with eagerness. I suspect on those evenings I was not around or a little tied up with work and thus could not extend the offer of tea and 'bikkies' they were disappointed.

I remember little of our conversations in the flat during those many late evenings. I know they would then go to bed, and so could I knowing that all was well. I just hoped I had helped.

FVH Unexpected Naked Boys

Despite my policy of not viewing naked boys, in a hostel of eighty or so young men, that policy did not always work out. The boys rarely covered themselves when walking to the showers, and the dorm doors were, for safety reasons, never closed. So staff walking past the dorms to their accommodation in Fort House would regularly have the vision of naked boy bums or full frontals. The boys never seemed to care about being seen in the nude. It was part of hostel life. They showered or bathed daily in front of each other. Why should it be different for staff?

The new bathing regime in Tower House made it a little tricky to monitor dormitory or bathroom events. On one occasion I was checking the dorm and surrounds. I had no idea I would find two boys in a bath together. It was, on their part, a time saving system. Neither of them showed the slightest concern at being seen naked by a teacher. I remember a very short polite conversation on my part before I scuttled away leaving them to continue their wash.

There was a local Junior school teacher of whom I was rather fond. We had been really rather naughty and rash, and skinny dipped at the local pool one warm night. As far as I know the only person who knew about our escapade was a trusted Head Prefect, Burton. That lovely lady eventually married someone else with the same surname, spelled a little differently—MacK . . . rather than McK . . . . [If she ever reads this she will know who she is. I just hope I will not be sued.]

She had visited me one evening after work. I had to check on some Tower hostel staff upstairs. Jane came with me. To my surprise a senior lad came out of his dorm on the way down to another dorm for his bath. He was stark naked except for the towel he had around his neck. Spotting the rather pretty J he faced her, stopped, and posed for her displaying his wares. I just caught sight of this, but was not immediately focussed on his face. I was more concerned about my lady friend. I should have had him whacked, but it all happened so quickly and surprisingly that I could not work out who it was.

J was, in any case, amused and flattered. "Cheeky monkey," she said. One has to laugh at the boldness of that young man. He knew that if I had caught up with him he would have been in trouble.

A rather naughty young man taking a risk. A good laugh all round.

Barry J Stone

FVH Old Master Prints

The hostel had been bludgeoned into a full repaint. What it needed was some cultural decor.

My parents lived in Salisbury (named after Lord Salisbury) later to be renamed Harare which has a bit of an unfortunate meaning. Visits north were as regular as possible. After so-called 'Independence' and the start of the tyrannical dictatorial rule of the sinister and evil Mugabe there were no more call ups, hence school holidays were free of the ordeal and drudge of police reserve duties.

During those days Educational Services loaned prints of paintings—Rembrandt, Constable, Turner, Da Vinci, Klee and so on—to schools for a term.

Taking advantage of this very valuable service, at the end of the holidays in Harare, I collected my first batch of paintings, about 12 to 15 in all, and loaded them easily into my rather spacious Mercedes Benz.

Back at Tower I thoroughly enjoyed placing these pictures in strategic places around the hostel where there was maximum exposure. They brightened up the place, adding warmth and sophistication. The hope was that the boys would learn something about art and discover the joy of art.

At the end of term all the pictures were packed into the car and driven to Harare. A visit to Educational Services for picture exchange expanded the scope of art in the hostel. It was a simple thing to do.

It mean that Tower House residents would have exposure to some more good, or at least famous artists. Whether this made any difference to their lives is a matter of speculation and history. I have no way of telling.

But a couple of years later the school was informed that those pictures were meant for the whole school, not just Tower House. I cannot remember what I did next, but I had initiated the art exchange programme and I felt that my hostel deserved the benefit. Nobody else in the school had done anything about it.

In any case I had resigned from Fort Victoria High in order to return to England. I have no idea what happened about the picture exchange programme.

FVH Guarding Devuli Bridge

One rather tedious aspect of being called up was that some military roles of the Police Reservists were little more than guarding bridges. I had been called up to guard Devuli Bridge, a bridge across a river in the East. The bridge was named after Devuli Ranch. No doubt by now the former white farmers have been killed or evicted with one hour to pack and go. The labourers would have been beaten up. The ranch will have become totally unproductive. The farm school will have closed.

But in the late 70's, with terrorists all about, various installations and constructions needed defending. Devuli bridge was remote, but there was a village on the other side of the river and a short distance downstream. Not visible from the camp which was basically a large living room tent joined to a cooking tent. A short distance across, and inside a fairly deep ditch, a large sleeping tent. A shower cubicle between constructed out of corrugated iron.

The tour of duty was four weeks, covering Christmas and New Year. Then back to school.

We had an small army truck (known as a bakkie, pronounced bucky) and so some of us could drive to the nearest small town from time to time to pick up a few supplies, which were very limited, from the few shops there. I remember tins of cool drink spaced out on the shelves in one row just to make the shop seem as if it had something in stock. That journey was nerve wracking in that we travelled at high speed on a bumpy road and so those of us on the back of the truck had to cling onto each other's clothing tightly lest we got bounced out at 70 mph. But it was a trip away from the tedium of the camp. At one time one of my younger departmental school staff was on the bakkie, but was in danger of being bounced out due to the speed and the crowded back of the bakkie. He asked me to hold onto his uniform tightly and I told him I would. I did. He did not fall out.

Later that tedious week he asked me to see what was wrong with one of his testicles. Probably a minor cyst. I told him what I suspected, and said I was not going to touch him in that area. I was not a doctor, and a doctor needed to check it out—not me. But I was touched that he felt safe to tell me of his problem.

During night watches I had a later guard duty, so could take early sleep until then. I had just dropped off to sleep and was shocked awake because of automatic fire just next to the tent. I grabbed my rifle which was next to me and fearfully emerged from the tent. It turned out that we were not under attack. A cobra had fallen into the deep ditch, was trapped, was seen, and then shot dead with automatic fire—probably in panic. A well aimed single shot would have disposed of the snake, and save much wasted ammunition. Such are the hazards of bush life. The most harmless animals were the numerous mice which were trying to raid our food supplies. Their numbers were reduced over time as we trapped them with rat traps bought in that small town. I never liked killing wonderfully constructed creatures, but they were a threat to us. Such it is in a fallen world.

I volunteered to do a daily burn of the camp refuse. This entailed taking the rubbish from the camp to a fire pit some way from the camp. A few cups of petrol. Then, standing back, throwing in a lighted match. Whoof! And the refuse burned. In those camps weeks I was working through the Old Testament. The daily fires in the refuse pit reminded me of the fires used for sacrifice in the temple courtyard. I often stood watching for a while. When the fires had cooled by the afternoon shovelfuls of ash were thrown down the long drop toilet, which was located some distance from the camp. The ash killed the smell. The long drop was a place for quiet contemplation.

The daily routine was simple. Breakfast. Ablutions. Shower. Rifle practice. Luncheon. Afternoon nap when not on duty. Supper. Conversation. Bed.

Interspersed within all this was guard duty—day shifts and night shifts. Always two or more on guard watching by night during the ephemeral moonlight; always listening. One soon got used to the sounds of the bushveld when darkness had fallen. The days rolled into weeks and soon the month was gone. I learned not to fret but to live existentially; not thinking about home, school or anything else. Just about the task in hand.

That region of Rhodesia is very hot. Most of the time we wore only shorts during the day. The morning ablutions were followed by the shower near the camp. Many of us walked naked to the long drop 100 m away wearing only boots, but carrying our rifles. Then back to the shower, boots off, rifle just outside the open shower cubicle and a shower fed by a water tank into which groundwater was pumped. Being near the river meant that the well did not have to be too deep before reaching the water table. Many was the time we showered with scorpions close by. We would kill them if we could. Magnificently designed creatures, and a shame to destroy such masterful engineering, but they could cause severe pain and sometimes death and we were far from a hospital.

For toilet not needing the long drop we had a so-called 'desert lily'. This was a tube with a funnel at the top pushed into the sandy soil. Much like a crude urinal. The 'lily' was moved regularly to avoid an unhealthy build up of urine in the soil.

Two weeks into my shift there was a change of reservists. Two were staff from Fort Victoria High—one a member of my department. I was glad to see them. They were clever enough to set up a two inch pipe under a canvas sheet at the road side of the camp. It looked like a heavy cannon. It 'aimed' at the bridge. They even covered the end with a sock—common practice to stop wasps making home in the barrel. We did something similar with our rifles using condoms, which would not prevent firing.

One new chap was rather well bred, a good conservationist, intelligent, and whose first question having greeted those of us in camp was, "Where is the-um—sand box". Well, I have heard the WC called many things: Loo the most common; the Necessarium; the Euphemism—but sand box was a new one.

One chap was a short stubby intellectually challenged braggart who knew everything about everything. A right royal pain in the ash-laaf. 'El Thicko' was the name some of us called him.

A third was a loud mouthed crude, rather nasty Australian. His only reason for being in Rhodesia was the war. He had a murderous heart itching to kill blacks. So he flew over and joined the police reservists. He had a foul mouth filled with blasphemy, swearing, and obscenities. Some of his favourite phrases could not be published in a book like this.

We had contact with central command and with our vehicles via short wave radio which was always on. All military vehicles had similar radios. All radio transmissions were monitored, not only by the Rhodesian authorities, but also by the Americans and perhaps the British and South Africans. Hence anything transmitted over the radio intelligence was heard by many ears. 'Rude Crude' had been out in the truck and about five miles from camp called in. He used the most putrid and disgusting language over the radio announcing his imminent arrival. I waited until he had finished, and then calmly broadcasted a sincere apology for the behaviour and language of the last caller with the Australian accent, affirming that none of us at Devuli Ranch had any association or agreement with that man. I knew he was listening.

When he got into camp he was rather sheepish and subdued and stopped his bad language for the rest of the time I was there. Sometimes it pays to gently chastise people who blaspheme and swear.

The villagers across the river would sometimes herd their cattle across Devuli bridge in order to allow them to graze on fresh unused grass on our side of the river. That grassland was not part of the ranch. They were not a threat, and they were relatively poor. Their livelihood was in their cattle. None of us minded at all, and it was good to see a bit of animal life on the other side of the road. Those villagers did not want the war any more than we did.

But then El Thicko arrived. When he saw the cattle he mercilessly gunned two of them down. It was a wicked act, evil to the poor creatures, and devastating to their innocent owners. His motive? To teach the villagers a lesson about not bringing cattle over to 'our side' of the river.

Within days the carcases began to rot and stink. The camp ponged when the wind came our way—which was most of the time. I wandered over the road a few days after the killing to see what was happening. Both cows were covered in fly maggots crawling around in what was soon becoming rotting exposed flesh. Soon they would pupate and emerge as swarms of flies. Normally those dead animals would have been quickly consumed by carnivores and vultures. But the presence of the camp and human beings seemed to keep them away.

We attempted to burn those carcases using diesel as a firelighter. But it did not work. They simply would not burn. Too moist. The only way would have been to pile them up and under with dry wood. There was none close by and nobody wanted to go too far from camp for fear of ambush.

About nine days later I returned to Fort Victoria leaving El Thicko to his stench and maggots and flies. Poetic justice. But a major economic loss the owners of the cattle. No wonder many black people hated whites.

In all the time we were at Devuli Ranch we did not have a single incident or encounter with terrorists. A few days after our return we heard that the camp had been attacked and shot up during the night. The hapless reservists called for assistance by helicopter gun ship. The response was that the helicopters did not fly at night, and that they would fly by at dawn to see if there was anything left. I never heard whether there were any casualties, but if there were I know who I would have liked it to have been.

I have always wondered why we were never attacked. Eight police reservists would have been easy pickings for a band of terrorists, especially at night.

I put it down to Divine Protection.

FVH Watertower Excursions

One tedious aspect of hostel life was the general drudge of being stuck at school and in hostel for weeks. The teachers had cars and could get out and about. But the kids were stuck. They were allowed out to walk to Friday youth groups, and walk to church on a Sunday, or with permission go into town, or take a walk in the local bush in small groups. Of course there were Saturday sports trips. And some were fortunate enough to have local relatives and trusted friends who could take them out on a weekend, or a Sunday if they had Saturday matches. But other than that the boring tedium routine of hostel and school life.

They did not have to have enhanced criminal record disclosures as in England where trusted friends are not allowed to take children out. The world of Rhodesia had a little more sanity and common sense.

As superintendent of Tower House or any hostel one is *in loco parentis* along with all supervising staff.

Nearby Fort Victoria is a kopje (hill) upon which is a water storage tank. But the kopje was a haven of peace and a little away from the school.

So, on my non duty evenings, I would collect a few boys into my large silver grey Merc and drive them up to the kopje to watch the sun go down. The Merc could fit six smaller boys or four bigger lads with ease.

Our excursions to the kopje were timed to always be back in time for the evening meal. But since they had been with me they were protected from any disciplinary action if we were a little late.

Climbing up the kopje was a bit of fun and exercise and a little more interesting than sitting around the hostel.

And then there was the sunset. The beautiful sunset. At that time of day the sunlight was filtered through the thicker horizon atmosphere and of course dust in the air. One could look at the sun directly without harm. There was no danger of going blind since the atmosphere and dust reduced the harmful rays to nothing.

We often timed how long it took from the moment the sun touched the horizon to final disappearance.

There is no way of assessing whether those late afternoon trips were appreciated. I would like to think so. They appeared to be popular. I tried to rotate the boys so that everyone had an opportunity. The Merc could as mentioned hold up to six passengers—especially small ones, although I tried to take a senior or two to keep the youngsters in order and to foster better relationships.

Occasionally I would take a couple of three staff up to the hill without the boys. That meant Marsala wine in crystal glasses. In those days having had a couple of 'toots' would not have been a problem. These were days of common sense and fun and minimal interference by authorities. Besides, the roads were quite clear most of the time.

Those were days of more relaxation between hard work; less stress; more laughter; more happiness; more fellowship and more fun.

Pity it is not much like that in 2014.

FVH The Horseshoe Braai

One wonderful aspect of African life is being able to spend much time outside. Another aspect is the braaivleis, shortened to braai. It is what other countries call a barbeque. I do not know the origin or meaning of the term barbeque, but *braai vleis* means burned meat.

Many hostel dwellers came from farms, most with permanent braais as part of the permanent outside structure. So to have a braaivleis evening would feel homely thus good for the boys.

To hold a braai for 80 or so kids presents certain logistical difficulties when there are only two of three braai fires, often oil drums cut in half longways with air holes punched into the bottom, and a wire mesh over the top. At Fort Vic High these were stored away, and had to be collected, set up, and returned the following day when they had cooled down. It was a performance.

So I came up with the idea of having a permanent brick braai, set a little away from the front of the hostel to reduce smoke wafting into to windows.

I commissioned one of the ground staff to build it. The inside diameter of the brick braai was about five metres. The width of the fire trough about 3/4 of a metre outside that. It was shaped like the letter C, in other words the shape of a horseshoe so that easy entrance could be gained. The idea was that people could cook from the inside of the braai as well as the outside.

The C construction was ready and dried out within three weeks. The grids had been commissioned from town. It was time to plan our first Saturday evening braaivleis. The ever caring cook matron Mrs Louw organised the meat and had the kitchen staff make plenty of traditional *sadza* (mealie meal cooked in saucepans with a little salt and the initial water added slowly until the porridge was cooked but stiff.) The mixture is heated and stirred continually, adding water slowly as the maize meal absorbs it and swells. Eventually one obtains the perfect stiff condition, not unlike mashed (not creamed) potato—delicious with an onion and tomato 'relish', also supplied by the kitchen.

Sports finished, travellers home, showering and bathing finished, a change into civvies. In the meantime some of the lads had set the fires, loaded the trough with charcoal, a left the fires to burn until they were hot glowing non smoking coals. Bottles of water at the ready to splash a little onto flames which may have arisen from fat catching alight. (It is traditional to use beer for that job—but we could not take a risk.)

Ready to go. Meat seasoned with a little salt. Let the mayhem begin. A few hostel staff eagerly joined in.

But there was one difficulty I had not anticipated. The heat in the middle of the braai was so intense that nobody could cook from the inside. We had to share the outside.

The positive things were that a community spirit evolved as the older boys helped the younger boys, and cooking in a circle made things very congenial.

FVH Table and Books in Foyer

Quite by co-incidence (or God-incidence as some would say) I chanced upon a huge eight legged table that the local library was donating to the school. And I happened to be walking through the forecourt to the main office when it was being unloaded.

No-one there seemed to know what to do with it. I seized the opportunity and exclaimed, "I'll take it!"

And so we acquired a very nice spacious table which could fit neatly into the main foyer of Tower House without obstructing passage. And that was where the young kids and the boys with special needs sat. Away from the restrictions of the prep room which meant an hour sitting in miserable silence with little to occupy their minds once they had finished their small amount of homework.

Although the foyer led through to the prep / dining area, the table was out of sight, so the foyer boys were able to move around a little and even communicate quietly. If they had homework they would tend to get it done because they were responsible to their teachers. My job, *in loco parentis*, was to encourage them to get their work done but within a comfortable and free environment.

There was a fairly long but empty bookshelf in the foyer and I was determined to fill it with books those boys might enjoy. I also wanted them to learn without pressure and practise, thus improve their reading skills. I asked the library for any books they were removing, and they gave me quite a few, but not enough to fill the bookcase. In my routine end of term newsletter I appealed to parents and guardians to obtain and rummage for suitable books they thought they could give away to the hostel. The response was very encouraging and the bookshelf was soon filled with novels, story books, non-fiction, science, history, sport, puzzles, games, picture books and a whole lot more.

This meant that those bored boys around that table had something to do when their prep was finished. The fidgeting declined, as did the need to talk.

Happiness.

FVH Smashed armchairs coming out of the Drive-In

We had a Drive-In cinema just out of Fort Victoria town. From time to time I drove the school mini bus with some senior boys from Tower House hostel to see a film. They could sit in the bus or bring blankets and sit on the ground close to the loud speakers placed on posts at each car parking space. Africa was fairly warm on a summer's January eve. I decided to take a couple of armchairs from the hostel—one for me and one for an accompanying member of the hostel staff whose name I would rather forget (ask me about it sometime). The boys strapped these armchairs to the top of the bus.

We drove through the entrance, paid for the show out of hostel funds, and found our ideal spot. When the show had ended, the armchairs were strapped back on top of the bus.

What I did not realize was that the gantry across the exit was lower than the gantry over the entrance.

So when we drove out the armchairs hit the exit gantry with a horrific crash smashing the chairs, scattering debris all over the driveway, and blocking exiting traffic.

Some of the lads leaped out of the bus and collected all the wood and debris they could find, loaded it into the bus, and off we went. We laughed all the way back to the hostel.

I don't think we ever put those chairs back together.

FVH Hippos at Lake Kyle

Lake Kyle was a local lake which I regularly visited. A beautiful lake where my lady friend and I sometimes went for a picnic and a bottle of wine.

The lake is fairly close to Fort Victoria and thus the school and hostels. In Europe and other places many lakes are surrounded by dwellings and facilities. Lake Kyle had but a few cottages. The rest was like most of Africa: free from human habitation. Upon one weekend when I was off hostel duty and Gillian was on duty I decided to take the senior prefects out for an overnight camp under the stars on a small island close to the shore of the lake.

The prefects readily agreed to a camp out. Anything to get away from the confines of the hostel. So, leaving the sub-prefects and a trusted member of staff in charge, we set out with food, drink, and cooking facilities. Plus, of course, sleeping bags.

There had been a drought, the waters were low, and it seemed almost possible to drive right up to the mini island. The island had become part of a temporary peninsula. But the Merc got stuck in the sandy muddy quagmire in the attempt to drive across to it. We had to use sticks and grass and people power to shove the motor car back towards the drier shore.

What a performance that was. At least we escaped being trapped without a car with a difficult journey back home, and a call-out to a motor car recovery service. I was not even sure their was one in town.

Leaving the car near the other shore behind, we carried our supplies and equipment onto the eastern side of our mini island, and set up what could loosely be termed 'camp'. It was still the dry season so tents were unnecessary.

I had previously offered to purchase that particular island from the widowed lady who owned it and the adjacent land. Her husband had died a while back. She refused my offer on the grounds that there was a Fish Eagle nest in one of the trees there. I really respected her for that decision. She must be long gone, but the fish eagles will still be around and about.

The lads swam naked in the warm waters of the lake. I was a little nervous as there were crocodiles further along. Little did I know that there was another, much more serious, danger in those waters. I started to cook supper whilst the boys dried off and dressed. We ate. Meals cooked in the open always seemed to taste better. Sunset was on its way.

After supper and after the large camp fire was lit we retired to our sleeping bags and bedded down for the night under the dark moonless but star-filled African sky which I always loved. We all chatted for a while. The hostel seemed 'long ago and far away.'

Being an oftimes insomniac and light sleeper I was awake to the sound of a hippopotamus just beyond the flames of the fire, in the water. He or she would have been rather annoyed by our presence because Hippo come ashore at night to graze. These are the most dangerous of creatures of the lakes and rivers of Africa. They are more likely to attack without provocation. Crocodiles, being reptiles, usually strike only for food. If they are not hungry they will leave you alone, unless provoked. Hippos are vegetarians, but capable of crushing human beings in their massive jaws. I have see photographs of people attacked in the rivers in a game park local to Giyani in the then northern province of South Africa.

The beast stayed put. The fire would have kept it at bay. Dawn emerged. I decided it to be circumspect and return home. The hippo was nowhere in sight; probably decided to feed elsewhere. We hastily moved ourselves to the car, away from danger, and took an early journey back 'home'.

I was sad to leave such a tranquil spot, but glad to be away from the beast and its compatriots.

FVH Fifth Brigade

In or around 1982 we were beginning to hear some alarming things. The country was now independent and renamed Zimbabwe. Robert Mugabe was the new Marxist Prime Minister having stolen the election, by intimidation, from the God fearing Bishop Abel Muzorewa.

In the Fort Victoria suburbs was a regular weekly Bible study and prayer meeting. It was held in the home of a married couple who were both missionary doctors. They were in contact with the nuns in the region. They were telling the doctors of shootings and killings where whole villages were being wiped out.

It was clearly the work of Mugabe and his military. A means of intimidation and thus control. And perhaps punishment for those who were perceived not to have voted for him.

We had learned that Mugabe had brought North Korean soldiers to Zimbabwe to train a large group of Zimbabwean recruits in terrorist tactics. They were to become his own special force called the Fifth Brigade, set up in 1981 and disbanded in or around 1987 or 1988 after many acts of murder and atrocities. Many thousands of innocent people, mainly Matabeles, were tortured and killed. The fifth brigade was answerable directly to Mugabe, and were not a part of the regular army. The fifth brigade had their own caps and uniform.

Thus we saw the start of a violent dictatorship which has ended in the torture and deaths of many. The Catholic Commission estimated conservatively that 20 000 people were murdered. Others estimated that number to be 30 000. Thus began the destruction of a once beautiful nation, rampant racism against whites and anyone not of the 'correct' tribe, and the ruination of what was once a thriving economy.

Zimbabwe has indeed become fully identified with the place of the origin of the Zimbabwe bird which is part of the Zimbabwe flag: The Great Zimbabwe ruins.

Libya and Syria come to mind.

FVH Name Changes

Britain was once occupied by the Romans, about two thousand years ago. A thousand or so years later the Normans conquered the country imposing their particular stamp of civilization. I live near a town called Staines which is one of the oldest Roman towns on the famous river Thames.

Britain has kept the names of those times, Roman names, Norman names. The only new names are mainly for new towns and establishments. This seems, to me, a mark of maturity and a sensible perspective of the past. A retention of history. And these days the studies of Roman and Norman times has greatly enriched our understanding of our culture and heritage. There has never been a time when names were changed just because we were annoyed and suppressed by our conquerors.

Yet in Africa there has always been a rush to change names of towns, cities and streets as quickly as possible after independence. In Zimbabwe this has been expensive using resources which could have been better used in more worthwhile projects such as helping the economy; job creation; schools; improvements in hospitals; and a host of other more worthwhile and useful projects than name changes.

Furthermore, for a while nobody knew where anywhere was. What effect did this have on tourism one wonders?

Fort Victoria had a name change. At first it was renamed 'Nyanda'. It turned out this was objectionable to the local people. The word nyanda meant soiled women's underwear which was the euphemism for sanitary towels.

So the town was renamed Masvingo.

So Fort Victoria High School became Masvingo High School. Somehow the classiness and dignity of being associated with a respected Monarch and Empress has been lost.

The Glenlivet Evening meal

Upon one occasion I treated the four senior hostel prefects to an evening supper at the Glenlivet hotel. That was near lake Kyle and also close to the Zimbabwe ruins. Therefore we were a few miles from Fort Victoria.

They deserved a treat having done a very good job in Tower House. It was a good hotel with good food and was fairly posh. I doubt whether it still exists. Such may be the ravages of the new regime.

It was a nice evening with a nice meal, and we were able to chat about several mutually interesting topics. Naturally the hostel came up, but I wanted to steer clear of school talk, and get to know these young men better. I enjoyed myself, and I think they did too.

I cannot remember them having much alcohol—perhaps a beer, but I had a couple of three or four drinks. I realized that it may put their lives in danger if I drove them back. Even though I could function as a slightly tipsy driver, and even though the roads would be quiet, I decided I would let one of the prefects drive back.

I settled on a certain A Beverley to take us home. I cannot recall whether he had a driving licence, but I think he did. People could get a full driving license at age 16 in those day. Even if he did not have a license he was old enough to drive. The chances of being stopped by police was close to zero. If it happened I would talk my way out of it.

He was the littlest youngest looking prefect, but I knew he had been taught to drive his father's Mercedes from an early age. In those times most kids were able to drive cars and other motorized vehicles long before the legal age (sixteen), and for good reason. Safety. Rural kids could drive people who needed to be driven to doctors and hospitals if necessary. My Godchild niece knew how to drive way before the legal age, and at age 15 would illegally drive her mothers Mercedes SLC to a mutual friend in the suburbs of Pretoria. A bit of make up and a scarf would mean she was never stopped. Hence she drives well now.

But one could do things in Africa which could not be done in Britain.

Beverley was one of my favourite young men since he was so good and kind and polite and nice, and he had a sense of humour. He was, despite his diminutive appearance at that time, sensible and mature beyond his age.

I sat myself in the back of the Merc because I wanted a front seat driver to wrest control if necessary. It was not necessary. I remember sitting comfortably in the quietness enjoying the idea that one of my lads was driving me home. It was a warm feeling being able to put my trust in a pupil, and not having to be the person in control.

Mr B brought us all home to the hostel perfectly safely.

Blyde River Canyon Trip

A trip to Blydepoort was arranged with a planned three day walk through the Blyde River Canyon.

I cannot remember how many of us were on that trip. There were three members of staff: Val Mogg, Rob Bailey, and me. We all took our own vehicles. The pupil complement could not have been more than about 10.

We had booked rooms for a night in the Blydeport hotel which was at the end of the trail two nights three days from the start of the hike. All three vehicles drove to the start of the trail, about 25 minutes by road from the hotel, but a three day hike through the canyon, with two nights in huts. All the kids were dropped of at the start of the trail with Val looking after them. Rob and I drove in two cars back to the hotel, and Rob left his campervan in the hotel car park. (In those days, in that place, vehicle theft was never a serious issue.) We both drove back in my Toyota Crown. Leaving the two vehicles at the start of the trail, we began the hike.

The plan was that when we reached the hotel at the end Rob would drive Val and me back to the start so he and I could pick up our cars. It meant leaving the kids unattended, but the older young ladies and gentlemen would look after them. Besides, there were the hotel staff, and in any case the team all needed a good bath and would be too pre-occupied to cause nonsense. They were responsible mature minded high school kids, otherwise we, the three staff, would not have invited them along to a possibly hazardous excursion. We would be gone for less than an hour. In any event nothing happened.

Both Val and I had packed our evening drink of choice. I took a full light plastic container of Masala sweet wine. Val took along a third of a bottle of gin in its heavy glass Gilbeys bottle. I never understood why he would want to hoick a heavy glass bottle around in his rucksack on a three day hike.

The scenery of the canyon was beautiful. It was good to be almost alone in the wilderness and wildness of that part of Africa. The kids were enjoying themselves. The hike on the first day was a gentle affair. A sandwich luncheon. Tea and coffee using clear crystal water from the river at the bottom of the canyon. We arrived quite early at the first hut. It had running water from a large storage tank, electricity and a hot tank. Rather luxurious considering where we were. Invisible staff would come in daily to top up the water tank using pumps down to the river, and would clean up the 'hut' ready for the next guests. In summer the hiking trail was fully booked with a daily stream of hikers we never saw.

Having arrived it was time to shower, change into some warmer clothes and cook. African nights in that part of the world can be quite chilly. Cooking outside was always a treat, even if it was on Calor gas single burners. The food always smelled and tasted better. We had some fresh meat for the first day, frozen at the outset, defrosted by the afternoon. After that it would be tinned and dried food.

A good night's sleep, up and dressed early for the hike, day two. A quick breakfast. Eggs and a carefully packed portion of a dry powdery apparently nutritious concoction with dried milk mixed in already. Add hot water to achieve an instant cereal meal that tasted awful, stuck stubbornly to the roof of one's mouth, and needed lots of sugar to swallow. But it kept us going until lunch break. I vowed that if we did this sort of thing again we would each take our cereal of choice. I would have chosen honey coated puffed wheat—something to look forward to.

Another beautiful day's hike with sunny blue skies and delightful sights, nice company, fresh air. Feeling good and healthy. Having 'warmed' up walk-wise the day before we made faster progress. Just as well the second hut was little further than the first hut was.

The second hut was just as nice as the first. The trail managers really knew how to look after their guests and understood the value of good publicity. By supper time day two it was clear that some of the kids were to running out of sugar. This was, for them, an unmitigated disaster. Tea and coffee and cereal without sugar? Bartering occurred. Sweets in exchange for sugar. Other foods too. We all went to bed early that evening. The trail map indicated the longest day's walk for day three.

Day three. 'Frodo' Mogg and I left much earlier than the rest who were fiddling around with ablutions and breakfast. A couple of the smaller boys came with. One of them was Glen Stephens I think. With the anticipated comforts of the hotel that evening we were inspired to put our best feet forward. But Frodo Mogg, being a 'large' gentleman, was having trouble with his knees. Our rucksacks were getting lighter as the food and fuel was consumed, but that heavy gin bottle, now almost empty, was a right royal drag. I would have drunk the whole lot of the gin on the second evening and dumped the bottle.

And so Val, myself, Glen and the other chap were slowed down. Rob Bailey took the rest of the group forward. Glen was about sixteen, and as said before, looked about fourteen because of diabetes, but had the mind of an eighteen year old. He appeared to enjoy adult company and despite his affliction was full of fun and cheer.

The slower pace suited me. Instead of forcing ourselves along we were able to enjoy the scenery.

Later that morning we were getting into pine forests. The trees were fairly spread out, so there was no difficulty in walking on the trail through.

A strange object resting on the forest floor appeared on our line of sight. Eagerly we veered towards it. Only when we reached it did we discover that it was a triangular support constructed of three sticks and some string. Suspended in the middle was a plastic bag, looking much like an icing bag for cakes. Within was what appeared to be a good pound and a half of white sugar. Some of the boys in the forward group had, as mentioned, run out of sugar and surely would have seen and investigated this strange 'apparition'. (The girls, ever watchful of their weight, would have taken the lack of sugar as a blessing in disguise. That, along with the hike, would have toned them up magnificently, and given them a better chance with prospective beaus.)

We were suspicious of the package. Obviously our scout compatriots were suspicious. Why would somebody leave precious sugar in the forest? What if the sugar was laced with some sort of poison? What if it was laced with crack cocaine or heroin to get us hooked so we become a market?

We passed on leaving the mystery package and wondering. Most likely the person or people carrying that sugar did not need it, did not want the extra weight and did not wish to waste it. An act of decency and charity and common sense. They could have just scattered the unwanted sugar over the forest floor for the ants. Perhaps a note of explanation would have helped

About two hours later, having cleared the pine forest thus walking in open flat grassland, we spied the hotel in the near distance. Joy. Soon we would be showering, bathing, soothing our sore feet, and tucking into a decent meal and a bottle of Chardonnay.

And then the chasm. What we did not know as we gleefully approached the hotel was that there was a steep fifteen or twenty metre gorge to negotiate between us and the hotel.

I decided that the two boys should go down first. They were lighter and more agile and could hold onto the branches of the reedy trees and bushes on the way down without destroying the route. They were down in quick time, and called up. I went down next, mainly sliding. Not many strong hand holds, so I was careful in my choice of vegetation to grasp. It took me much more time than to boys to slide down on my backside, feet trying to prevent moving too fast.

At the bottom of the gorge was a small shallow stream. It would be easy to cross.

Next came Val Mogg. We stood away from the end of the path down. Thus began a simultaneous conglomeration of swearing, grunting, ooh-ing, and aah-ing, accompanied with a landslide of stones and soil and dust, and leaves from the bushes and small trees raining down. Eventually Val arrived at the bottom, hot and sweaty having destroyed that particular section of flora and footholds. The next group would need to select another slither point.

Now came the climb out. We paddled across the stream and began our ascent. Firstly the two young lads. Again, for them, quick and easy. Then me. It was a strenuous climb—more difficult that sliding down. Selecting hand and foot holds needed to be done sensibly. I made it.

Poor Val took much more time, and did not have the breath to treat us to blasphemies and obscenities. The three of us at the top waited patiently for his emergence, even more dusty, hot and sweaty than before.

That evening we bathed well, ate well and slept well.

It is an interesting phenomenon that kids, having endured quite a considerable amount of inconvenience and hardship, confess (retrospectively) to having loved the entire experience.

Odd that.

Our departure the following morning required a packing up of rucksacks and other equipment into the three vehicles. I already had my uncomfortable borrowed second world war Y frame rucksack in the boot of my Toyota Crown.

But in the packing this was 'temporarily' taken out by my passengers and left on the embankment whilst they fitted in their large comfortable back packs.

Our next stop was Tshipise near the border of what had become Zimbabwe. The plan was for a soak in the hot mineral springs, a shower, a braai and an overnight camp. Which we did. When we arrived I realized that my rucksack been left behind. It was a sobering experience to be left only with the clothes I was wearing—not even a towel or comb. And no sleeping bag. Just shorts, short sleeved shirt and shoes. Fortunately it was warm. That night I slept in Rob's campervan.

I phoned the hotel from the office. They had the rucksack and promised to send it on to Fort Victoria with someone travelling north. This actually happened, but it arrived *sans* a jersey. It probably disappeared in Fort Victoria. I doubt whether anyone staying at the Blydepoort hotel would need a jersey. Ironically the Masala wine in the plastic container was left alone.

Strangely I quite enjoyed that existential experience of temporarily having nothing much. One thought of the millions of people who only had the clothes they were wearing. Some have even less. One of my enduring memories is a newspaper full page photo taken in or around 1992 of a starving very skinny totally naked teenage boy walking towards a refugee camp in the hope of gaining some food. He was looking directly into the camera. It was yet another African war situation. The caption was that the boy died three days after the photo was taken.

I sometimes think of that young man when I am thinking about feeling sorry for myself.

FVH *The Sixth Form Trip*

The sixth form won a school competition for the class that sold the most fund-raising raffle tickets. Against the odds as they were the smallest group in the school.

The reward: A trip to a hotel in the Eastern Highlands for a few days rest and rambling.

Fozia Dimiati was what we call in English parlance, 'A card'

Fragmentally wildly over weight. But great fun.

As we arrived to inspect our rondavel chalets Fozia walked in and the wag of a sixth former noticed a large round raffia mat in the middle of the living are. "Finally," he said, "A prayer mat big enough for Fozia." We all packed in laughing, Fozia included.

On the first evening, we dressed well for the evening meal. Fozia looked very glamorous. She was a good looking Arabic black Indian (I seem to remember) with glowing dark skin, and very sophisticated and from a wealthy family.

That first night we went for dinner in the hotel. As we all got out of the bus, I asked Fozia to stay with me whilst I locked the bus. I had hatched a joke.

We waited until the others were seated at the table. Then Fozia and I sauntered in arm in arm chatting away and pretending not to notice the other seated guests. Of course we did notice. The place had gone very quiet. Despite the New Zimbabwe, where racism was abolished, there was still racism among some. Some of the other guests had been horrified. A black woman with a white man!?

The rest of our party were in great mirth over this.

And so we spent the long weekend enjoying the facilities and the long walks though the forests of the Eastern Highlands.

FVH Regrets

The old song 'I did it my way' has a line about having regrets comes to mind. "Too few to mention."

It is probable that many people have regrets. [I never liked the Frank Sinatra song—and neither did he it seems. Wrong philosophy altogether.]

I record a few of my own.

I regret having caned some boys in my 'youth' as a young new teacher. I know some boys would be better off with the caning. That is scriptural. Spare the rod and damn the child. A man who does not beat his son hates his son. God disciplines us. But some boys did not need a caning.

I regret not talking through some disciplinary issues. Especially with intelligent teenagers. If I did it all again I would have conversed rather than caned. The most regrettable thing for me was that as a big strong man needing to be feared I whacked those poor boy's bums as hard as I could. I hope they can forgive me. I loved those kids.

I regret dissuading a father from driving a long distance at night see his son before he unexpectedly died in hospital. I hope he has forgiven me 30 something years on.

I regret not showing more compassion. It was not so much a lack of love and care as a British stiff upper lip reserve. Sometimes people, especially kids, need a hug. One cannot do this in England. The cry is, 'paedophile' or sexual abuse. Teachers often love their wards. Teachers also need a hug.

I especially regret the time I was phoned to inform me that one of my hostel lads sick mother had died. Remember that Fort Victoria was far from any other centres, hence the phone call but not a family visit.

I had to ask that poor young chap into the office. I was quite emotional and on the verge of breaking down. I sadly told him about his mum. He knew she was critically ill. He was silent for a few moments, and then burst into tears. I regret not taking him into my arms and comforting him. I regret not bringing him into the lounge and making him a cup of tea. I regret not remembering his name or what he looked like.

I regret not listening more to the kids, and forging ahead with my own plans and ideas. Youngsters need to be taken seriously. Know-it-all self-opinionated teachers are not a good idea. Some of the best, usually older and wiser, teachers I knew were listeners.

But despite regrets there were many good and positive times. Frustrating times, but mainly fun times. What started as a three year compulsory contract to fulfil an obligation to the Ministry of Education for awarding me a very good bursary for four years turned into more than seven years of hard work, personal growth, fun and enjoyment.